THE WORLD OF
FAIRIES

Dedication

In loving memory of my mother,
Ugunsmate of my heart.

THE WORLD OF
FAIRIES

GOSSAMER PENWYCHE

A GODSFIELD BOOK

First published in Great Britain in 2001 by Godsfield Press Ltd

A division of David & Charles Ltd, Brunel House,

Forde Close, Newton Abbot, Devon, TQ12 4PU

10 9 8 7 6 5 4 3 2 1

Designed for Godsfield Press by

The Bridgewater Book Company

Illustrations Sandy Gardner, Catherine McIntyre

Picture Research Lynda Marshall

Printed and bound in China

ISBN 1-84181-091-6

Acknowledgements

I wish to offer my heartfelt gratitude to Jane Alexander and Katey Day at Godsfield Press, as well as Sarah Bragginton and
Emily Wilkinson at Bridgewater Books, for guiding me on my profound and magical journey through *The World of Fairies*.
I would also like to thank Sandy Gardner and Catherine McIntyre for bringing that world to light with their beautiful
illustrations. More thanks go to Professor Frank Hoff and Velga Jansons for helping me with the ethnic and cultural
details. For their unfailing love and support, I thank my aunts Gita and Alma and family and friends too numerous to
name here. I am also indebted to Ian Jackson, without whom I may never have found the way.

CONTENTS

PREFACE

 I believe in fairies. My belief is based on a simple, childlike faith that I have never lost and a childhood experience I have never forgotten. I was in the woods that bordered the property of my childhood home. I was alone and unafraid, playing in one of my favorite haunts, a stream that lay in a hollow of one of the numerous waterfalls that can be found along the Bruce Trail of southern Ontario. It was midday and midsummer. The sun was at its highest point overhead but all was cool and green in the shady glen where I played. When a sudden gust of wind threatened to topple me off the rock where I stood in mid-stream, I sat down on a broad, flat stone that protruded several inches above water, providing me with a safe, solid cushion. I let my outstretched legs float freely in the cool water.

A sharp cry announced the arrival of a hawk. I turned my attention upward to an ancient oak whose longest branches extended almost halfway across the stream. The hawk had landed on the end of one of the lowest branches. A faint breeze started up again, whirling around me in circles, warm and embracing. I felt as if I were at the vortex of a small tornado, and began to sway in spiraling, synchronized motion with the wind.

Song birds, which had abruptly ceased to sing with the arrival of the hawk, began to chirp again, with increased fervor. Rising above the melodious chatter of the birds I could discern the sound of sweet, youthful voices singing a lighthearted tune. When the song ended, the hawk, still on its perch, let out another cry and stretched its wings to prepare for flight. It took off, flying directly toward me. The sight of the hawk's intense gaze approaching me in close, low-level flight was terrifying. I threw up my hands to protect myself just as the great bird suddenly veered upward to avoid colliding with my face. It came so close that I could feel the rush of its wings on my cheeks as it flew by me. My fear turned to amazement when I caught a glimpse of the hawk's large, fan-shaped tail. It looked like a feathered cape or the train of a doll's dress. I was so startled that I slipped off the rock and fell into the stream. I was certain that I heard children's laughter as I struggled to sit upright, waist high in water. I looked all around me for the source of the laughter but saw no one. I sat in the water for several moments as I tried to regain my composure.

When I finally came back to my ordinary senses, I noticed that the sun was no longer in its usual noon-day position, but was resting quite low in the western sky. Several hours had lapsed while I had noticed only a few minutes. Though I should have been puzzled by this strange revelation, I felt only profound disappointment. I wanted to be in that weird and wondrous place I had been in just moments before. I wanted the magic to return.

My fairy encounter, for I have no doubt that is what it was, has haunted me all my life. I still love to go for the long, desultory walks in the woods, always hoping to find some reaffirmation of my faith. Had it not been for that remarkable afternoon in the woods of my childhood, perhaps I would not believe so strongly in something I know exists just outside of my ordinary perception. It left me with a yearning that does not abate.

The result of my lifelong search to return to the fairy realm is the creation of this book. I have tried to describe a world much older than civilization and as elusive as a long-lost memory. It is a realm of wishing, longing, beauty, and terror. It is my hope that some of the words and images contained here will bring the reader closer to that world.

Blessed be.

INTRODUCTION

*T*he fairy realm is world where the unknown, unseen, intangible, and irrational operate as the norm. It has an internal logic all of its own. It is the first place pre-industrial peoples went to find explanations for the unexplainable. It is where science has no power and magic rules above all else.

Reports of fairy sightings are not nearly as numerous as they once were. Since the advent of the Industrial Revolution, encounters with fairies have become very rare, no doubt due to the fact that fairies fear iron (a good tool for warding them off) and detest large crowds. However, there are numerous accounts in the folklore of many cultures about mortals finding their way into the Otherworld. The journey to the other side is as illusive and problematic as the fairy realm itself, but there are some ways to gain entry if one knows where to look.

Gateways to the Otherworld can be accessed by mortals at times and places that are "in-between," neither here nor there, then nor now. Dusk, dawn, midnight, and midday are all times that lie between darkness and light, night and day, morning and afternoon, and are reputedly the most auspicious times for seeking the fay. A fork in a path or road, the banks of a river or stream, and the shores of a lake or sea lie "betwixt and between" one place and another, and are therefore favorable locations for fairy sightings. Secret worlds are also found in deep, dark settings such as forests, caves, and at the bottom of lakes and seas. Misty weather is highly favored by the fairy folk as well, because it enshrouds reality with a delicate, ever-shifting cloak, recreating the illusory worlds in which they dwell. Fairies are frequently reported to be seen by the pale light of the moon, especially when it is full. Folk and fairy tales abound with mortals who encounter fairies under these and similar circumstances.

Engaging in repetitive movement and sound is another effective way to gain entry into other realities. There are numerous accounts of mortals who have nearly danced themselves to death when they have been caught up in the ecstatic revelry of the Otherworld. The constant repetition of movement and sound weaves patterns, forming order out of randomness and chaos. Folk tales from around the world frequently feature fairies and mortals performing the highly repetitive, deceptively mundane tasks of spinning and weaving, which create invisible portals to other realms.

Fairies are immortals and have no need for linear, measurable time. A mortal in the fairy realm loses all sense of time and may return to this world after what seems like a few days, only to find that hundreds of years have passed. There are also tales that tell of the reverse, where days and months in the Otherworld are but a few moments here, and the effects on wayward mortals far less drastic, but these are the exception rather than the rule.

Despite their mistrust of most mortals, fairies tend to favor individuals who do not fit into mainstream society. This is due, in a large part, to the fact that they are outcasts themselves. When Christianity became the dominant religion of Europe, nature spirits and elementals were ever-present reminders of the deeply entrenched pagan beliefs it could not completely eradicate. So the church relegated fairies to the status of demons, or spirits of the dead, who were too good for hell and not good enough for heaven.

Thus, fairies appreciate and embrace the outsiders of mortal society. The mortals fairies traditionally support are mad people, fools and clowns, poets, artists, spinsters, widows, the very young and very old, homosexual men and women, and any other marginalized or disenfranchised people. It is especially appropriate that the ostensibly pejorative epithet "fairy" is applied to gay men. It is an irony that has not gone unnoticed by fairies of either this world or the other.

One of the most prevalent reasons for the marginalization of all things fairy by the church is their rampant sexuality. The fact is, fairies are a highly libidinous lot. There are legions of stories from various countries that describe mortal men overwhelmed with lust for an enticing nymph. A man who makes love with a female fairy invariably experiences a rapture he has never known with a mere mortal. Couplings between mortal women and male fairies are not as well documented.

That which is unknown and unnamed lies beyond the portals of the fairy realm. Time spent with fairies reveals knowledge and wisdom that is pre-verbal and unconscious. Following the way of the fay is not simple-minded escape from reality. It is a means of exploring another reality.

ABOUT THIS BOOK

*T*HE STORIES IN THIS BOOK are derived from a variety of sources. Most of them are retellings of famous and not-so-famous folk and fairy tales. Some of the stories are my own invention, based on traditional folk and fairy lore, and still others have been inspired by ideas or lines from works by fairy friendly writers such as Shakespeare and Yeats.

The stories were chosen to demonstrate the particular habits and behaviors of each of the twenty-nine fairies and the most common lessons learned by mortals who encounter them. I ascribed only one lesson to each fairy, although meeting up with a fairy usually provides more than one useful message for the wary mortal. For example, although I designated the lesson of seduction to the rusalki, there are certainly many other fairies from whom mortals may learn that particular lesson.

In selecting the stories it was my purpose to demonstrate the similarities, rather than the differences, of diverse fairy traditions. I also made an effort to use fairies from as many different cultures as possible. I discovered many highly developed spiritworlds in folk traditions I previously knew little about, but restricted the stories to those for whom I felt a comfortable familiarity, in order to best illustrate the lessons and the predominant themes outlined in the introduction. I sincerely apologize for my inadequacies as a chronicler of fairy-dom to all the vibrant, fairy-friendly cultures that I did not include, and especially to the fantastic beings that inspire them.

STAR MAIDEN

Grace

THERE ARE A MULTITUDE of legends from the native peoples of North America that describe the origins of nature's many wonders. Some of the most beautiful of these stories are about the night sky and its stars. The Ojibwa Nation of the Great Lakes region regarded the stars as good spirits who looked down from the Land of Stars and watched the daily affairs of their earthly neighbors without judgment or censure.

Star Maidens are radiant beings with long, coal-black hair and skin the color of burnished copper. They are spirits who are as kind as they are beautiful. In their earthly guise they have very long, pointed wings that glow a pale, silvery white. Like the stars in which they dwell, Star Maidens are only visible at night. Occasionally they will appear to mortals in their dreams. They are known to be very polite and will go to great lengths not to offend or disturb mortals.

Star Maidens teach us the lesson of grace. Grace is a heavenly blessing or Otherworldly charm that is manifested on the earthly plane as peace and beauty, whether it be in a person, place, or thing. Such grace does not fade with age or experience. Graceful, gracious people comfort others by their very presence.

You cannot harbor cynicism and grace at the same time. Look at your surroundings and other people as if it were for the first time, before worldly affairs and disappointments destroyed your childlike innocence. Grace is found in the purity of a child's soul. It comes from a clear mind and an open heart. Rediscover the innocent child you once were and there you will find grace.

The Star Maiden's Tale

THERE WAS A TIME, very long ago, when all the animals and people of the earth lived together in peace and harmony. Tribal war was unknown and the winters were mild and without hardship. The buffalo, elk, and deer lived without fear of man, for they understood the natural order of things, and were willing to sacrifice their lives for The People. Although there was more than enough food for everyone, hunters never took more than was needed to feed their tribes, for The People did not know greed. Birds sang more sweetly, children played more joyfully, and the rain fell softly upon the land. All that lived in or upon the earth was honored and revered.

Every night, after Father Sun had set, the people would gather around their campfires to celebrate life and honor the Great Spirit who had bestowed them with so much peace and beauty. They would tell their stories and smoke their pipes as they gazed up at the night sky, admiring the splendid Land of Stars that lay above them. The People believed that only the most worthy spirits deserved to live in such a vast and lovely land.

One moonless, summer night The People noticed a star that shone brighter than all the others, resting just above the southern horizon. The next evening the star was there again, glowing brighter than before. Night after night the star grew in magnitude, until a month had passed and the tribal chiefs met to discuss what the star might portend. Some thought it was a sign of good fortune, others thought it foretold evil. After many hours of deliberation, the elders were unable to come to any conclusion, so they decided to wait for another omen.

A few days later a young brave dreamed that a beautiful young woman visited him in his wigwam that night. She stood before him in a robe of white buckskin that cast a gentle glow all around her. Her long wings reached up to the top of the wigwam.

"I have come from the Land of Stars and I have been watching your people for many moons now," said the Star Maiden to the young brave. "There is much joy and laughter among you. It is my wish to come and live among your people. Please go to your wise men and ask them if I may do so." A moment later the lovely maid faded into the darkness.

The next morning the young brave went to the council of elders and told them of the Star Maiden's request. The elders were delighted with the news and burned sweetgrass and other fragrant herbs to welcome the young maiden. Smelling the sweet aroma of the burning herbs, the Star Maiden descended from her resting place in the southern sky and came to hover directly over the village. After a great feast in honor of the Star Maiden, the elders told her that she was at liberty to choose any place she wanted for her new home on earth. The elders believed that she would bring great blessings to The People, no matter where she dwelt.

And so the maiden began to search for her new home. At first she chose to live in a delicate wild rose that grew in the western mountains, but found that it was too far away from the people she so loved. Then she thought she might live in the tall grasses of the prairies, but feared being trampled by the hooves of the great buffalo. She tried staying on top of the rocky cliffs that overlooked the village, but worried that the children, whom she loved the most, would injure themselves when they came to visit. So the Star Maiden continued on her journey across the land until she saw some children playing on the shore of a sparkling, deep-blue lake that reminded her of the home she had left behind in the Land of Stars.

"This is where I shall live," announced the Star Maiden. "The children will keep me company and I can watch The People as they glide gently by in their birch-bark canoes." Then the Star Maiden spread her shining, white wings behind her and lay back upon the still waters. The next morning, as was their habit, the people of the village arose and came to the lake to wash. There, where the Star Maiden had lain upon the water, were hundreds of milk-white, star-bright water lilies, floating gracefully on the lake. Thus it was that the Star Maiden brought the radiant beauty of the Land of Stars to the earth and its people.

ASRAI
Vulnerability

ASRAI ARE VERY DELICATE, nocturnal water spirits who have been observed in the lake districts of Wales, the highlands of Scotland, and the English counties of Cheshire and Shropshire. Their skin has a pale, translucent quality that renders them almost invisible in the deep, dark waters where they dwell. When in human form they appear as very small, slight, adolescent females, although a few sightings of male Asrai have been reported. They are very elusive fairies who shun the company of mortals. The only thing they avoid more than human contact is the sun. Even the slightest exposure to sunlight will cause them to dissolve into a pool of water.

The fragile nature of the Asrai makes them one of the most vulnerable spirits in the fairy realm. Asrai remind us that vulnerability can be used as a strength and not a weakness. Although the delicate beauty of the Asrai makes them very appealing to mortals, more often than not it is their vulnerability that protects them from human encroachment. Their defenselessness usually turns away all but the most offensive, grasping humans. Only the most belligerent, insensitive mortals feel triumphant when they have used their power at the expense of another's vulnerability. Such behavior may serve a warrior in battle, but it does little to preserve peace and quiet for ordinary folk. By following the example of the Asrai, we are able to recognize the security and serenity of our vulnerability.

The Asrai's Tale

IT IS AN ANCIENT TRADITION for the fishermen of the borderlands of England and Wales to cast their nets onto lakes that glisten with the light of the full moon. The magical hours when the moon is full are times when fish rise to the surface to feed. But fish are not the only denizens who dwell in the deep and appear on moonlit nights. More beautiful than any fish are the Asrai, hundreds of years old and yet no more than children in bearing. Asrai have long lived in the dark of the waters and the dark of the night, and come into mortal sight only when the moon shines full and bright.

It was on just such a night that a fisherman caught a shy and gentle Asrai in his net. At first he knew not what it was that tugged and pulled on his nets with such force. He peered through the dark to where the splashing occurred, and there, in the tangled net, was a young girl. But what a young girl she was! She looked to be wearing a flimsy robe of seaweed, until he realized that it was her long, green hair that swirled in the waters around her. While dragging her onto his boat he wondered that she had any form at all, for he could not feel the weight of her in his net. As he struggled to pull the slippery spirit into his boat, he felt a sharp pain course through the palms of his hands, where he had touched her cold, wet skin. The pain felt at once like fire and ice, and caused him to pause briefly in his thoughtless task.

The Asrai entreated him to set her free but he would not, for she was the rarest and most precious creature he had ever seen, let alone captured in his nets. Her plaintive cries, however, moved him to pity, so he gently draped her trembling body with seaweed so fine that it was indistinguishable from her hair.

"This should keep her warm," he thought stupidly as he tucked the weeds around her. It was not the cold that made her shiver, however, but fear. "Such a creature as this is worth a thousand fish," he said aloud to himself, and began his journey back to shore. He had rowed his boat in the same manner a thousand times before, but on this occasion he labored more than ever, and still the boat would barely move. The more he toiled with his oars, the more the Asrai cried and moaned. The fisherman was most perplexed by how tiresome his task had become and how little headway the boat was

making. The oars felt as if he were slicing through molasses rather than water. And all the while the little fairy protested with squeals so shrill that he was forced periodically to cover his ears with his hands to dim the sound of her cries. He must have been a very dull man indeed, not to understand the reason for his inability to make such a simple journey. By the time he reached the shore it was almost dawn.

The Asrai had not ceased her wailing when at last the simple fisherman decided to relent and release her back into the lake. But, being a man who was as slow in his actions as he was in his wits, he was too late to save his hapless prisoner. Just as he was bending over to lift her out of the boat, the sun rose above the distant hills, and one of its rose-colored rays shone down upon the Asrai. At that moment she let out such an awful scream that the fisherman was knocked backward into the bottom of the boat. He lay there for several moments, even more dazed and befuddled than he was wont to be. When the fisherman returned to his senses and looked to where the Asrai had lain, he found only seaweed floating in a pool of water.

The fisherman was left with nothing for all his troubles but deep red welts upon the palms of his hands, where he had touched the Asrai. They remained there for the rest of his life, reminding him of his cruel and selfish deed.

CHANGELING
Survival

IN ORDER TO STRENGTHEN a sickly strain in their species, fairies sometimes steal robust, healthy, human babies and replace them with one of their own ailing children. Stories of these fairy replacements, called changelings, are widespread throughout Europe. The stolen mortal babies are substituted with ugly, malformed fairies that are a result of poor bloodlines due to inbreeding. Sometimes the changelings are nothing more than wooden logs, disguised as humans by fairy spells, that appear to wither and die soon after they have been discovered. Very old fairies, who are willing to be coddled by mortal parents, are known to have been substituted as well.

Numerous methods of getting rid of changelings and finding the real child have been tried over the years, many of them very cruel and injurious. As for the stolen children, they usually live very pampered lives among the fairies, who are grateful for mortal assistance in their species' survival.

While some mortals have the good fortune to ponder what immortality would be like, most struggle just to get through the day. Fairies, like animals (to whom they are more psychically connected than humans), are not burdened with issues of how or why they survive. However, mere survival is obviously not enough for humans, who aspire to much more than the daily grind.

Fairies respect and favor survivors, those people who overcome adversity. Survival, especially when it is particularly against the odds, happens with human will, perseverance, and perhaps a little intervention from the unseen world.

The Changeling's Tale

Gabi and Eric were the happiest couple in the land with the arrival of their first-born child, Little Eric. Long had they waited for that blessed day, and their joy knew no bounds when Little Eric was born healthy and sound. Within three weeks of his birth, Little Eric was christened by the village priest before family and friends.

There was much celebration and rejoicing in their home after the happy occasion of Little Eric's baptism. Everyone was happy, except for Little Eric, who was cranky and complained in the manner that infants do, with much boisterous weeping and wailing. Little Eric's father took it to be normal behavior from a child who had had to endure too many people and too much activity for one day. But the mother was not so sure. Gabi noticed that Little Eric seemed uncharacteristically out of sorts for a child who had demonstrated such a cheerful, wholesome disposition in the first days after his birth. She had her fears but she kept them to herself, pretending all was well.

The weeks passed and the happiness the new parents first felt at the birth of their son gave way to worry and vexation. Little Eric became the most cantankerous, ill-behaved child they had ever known, and it wasn't long before the unhappy parents wondered what they had done to deserve such a boy. Mother Gabi's suspicions increased as time passed. She was afraid to voice her fears aloud, and prayed daily that she was mistaken about her newborn child and his true condition.

Though he was born as handsome a child as any, by the time Eric was six weeks old his face had developed a permanent frown that made him look angry and old beyond his years. Worst of all was the child's appetite. Never had the couple known a small child to eat so much. Gabi and Eric were not poor people, but neither were they wealthy. Gabi struggled to keep up with the constant feedings. Little Eric was consuming as much milk and barley in a single day as his parents ate all week.

Fortunately, Little Eric had no regard for the quality of the food. His mother could place any ill-prepared, undercooked meal before him, and he ate it as if it were a feast. Gabi was grateful for this one small blessing, for she had no time to fuss over food preparation. By the time he was a toddler, running about the cottage and wreaking havoc everywhere, his distraught parents wondered why they had ever wanted to have a child at all. Mother Gabi's apprehension grew into certainty with every passing day, but still she kept her peace.

Indeed, if Gabi had seen how Little Eric behaved when no one was about, she would have known her suspicions were correct. Whenever Little Eric was left unattended, which happened more and more frequently as he grew older, he did the strangest things. He was able to climb up walls and across ceilings as if he were a squirrel in a tree. Sometimes he would hang upside down from the ceiling, laughing and squealing with delight at his topsy-turvy world. It was under just such circumstances that his mother found him one day. When she spied Little Eric blithely hanging from the rafters like a bat, Gabi knew at once that he was a changeling. It was just as she had feared all along.

All at once Gabi felt guilt and remorse for the loss of her real son. She remembered how, a few days after he was born, she had left him unattended in his crib. Some fairies had obviously seized the opportunity to steal her healthy son and replace him with an ugly changeling. He was alone for only a few minutes, but that would have been long enough since the child had not been baptized. Without further ado, and with no compunction whatsoever, Gabi prepared to get rid of the little fiend.

"No God-fearing household should tolerate such devilry," Gabi muttered to herself. With the help of the neighbor's daughter, she piled the hearth high with kindling, and then instructed the girl to light a fire so hot that no human could withstand it. Three times the girl asked Gabi why she did such a thing, and three times Gabi replied, "To burn the little demon who lives in our midst."

When the same answer was repeated a third time, a troll woman appeared at the door. In her arms she held a beautiful, mild-mannered little boy, whom Gabi recognized at once to be her own son. The troll woman grabbed the changeling from Gabi and placed the real Little Eric on the floor.

"There's your child for you. I have treated him much better than you have mine," cried the troll mother.

Indeed, Little Eric was hale and hearty, and did not appear to have suffered at all for his abduction. He was baptized straightaway and grew up to be a handsome, clever young man, with more charm than any one mortal deserved.

DEETKATOO

Patience

THE TILLAMOOK INDIANS OF the American Northwest used seashells as their principle form of currency, which is why the benign, passive spirits known as the Deetkatoo have been observed to grow seashells on their bodies. The Deetkatoo are usually under three feet tall and dwell deep in the rainforests of the northwestern United States.

To find a Deetkatoo is considered very lucky, because they will bestow good fortune upon the mortals who find them, provided they are treated with respect and the proper protocol, a feature shared by many fairies throughout the world. They are usually found in the earth and, like the trees and plants that surround them, will flourish and spread the benefits of good care and health to their mortal neighbors. Similarly, like their herbaceous companions, if they do not receive proper sustenance and guardianship, they remain inert and unproductive, thus depriving mortals of their potential blessings.

The Deetkatoo embody the essence of life in a pristine, natural environment. To reap the rewards offered by these fairies, mortals must slow down and live at the speed of nature. Patience is a virtue that is disappearing even faster than the rainforests. The pace at which mortals live in our highly technological world has created a society out of touch with the cycle of the seasons, and the gradual processes of nature, which define the true speed of life.

Take time out from the fast-paced, high-tech world and return to nature. Like giant fir trees that have stood for hundreds of years, ostensibly doing nothing, reaching maturity and finding peace is a gentle process, and one that requires infinite patience.

The Deetkatoo's Tale

IN THE GREAT FORESTS of the Pacific Northwest there once lived a very poor family. There were Mother, Father, and their two children, Son and Daughter. They were much like many other families who lived in the village, until one day Father went away. He secretly stole away one night. He was weary of poverty and hardship, and thought he could do better on his own.

So Mother took her children and moved in with her two married brothers. Life was hectic for Mother, but she did the best she could. While her brothers went out fishing during the day, she would wander in the woods looking for food. Every day she would hunt for berries and edible roots. She worked so hard that sometimes she would forget to eat, and at other times she did not eat on purpose so that there would be more for everyone else. Her life was thus for many moons. She sacrificed much, received little, and never complained.

There came a day when she was digging in the earth for fern roots. Every time she threw away the earth she had dug up, she heard a faint cry. No matter how hard she looked she was unable to find out who or what was crying. Although she looked as much as she dug, she went home that evening none the wiser, and very puzzled about her day.

After a restless night, the next day Mother returned to the same place to look for the mysterious source of the crying. She went about her business as she had the day before and, sure enough, each time she threw some dirt she heard a little wail. Mother took her time and kept an eye on the spot where she cast the dirt. Then she saw him. Buried under the pile of earth she had built was the Deetkatoo.

Ever since she had been a young girl Mother had heard stories of the magical Deetkatoo, so she knew exactly what to do. He was a little person, no higher than her knees. Ever so gently Mother picked up the hairy little Deetkatoo and wrapped him in her cloak. While billing and cooing to keep him calm, she put the little thing into a hole in the ground. To keep him hidden and protect him from the rain, she covered the pit with a layer of sticks and leaves. Finally, with a fresh bunch of delicate fern roots in her arms, she returned home. She handed the pile of fern roots to Daughter and instructed her to help her aunts fix up something for everyone to eat. "As for me, I'm going to bed," said Mother, "I don't feel well."

True to her word, Mother retired to her bed and there she remained. She ate not a morsel of food the whole time she was there. Her brothers and children worried about her. Try as they might they could neither persuade her to eat nor get out of her bed.

On the third day, before the others had awakened, Mother stole away to inspect the Deetkatoo. His fine, black hair had already begun to turn into delicate seashells. Without stopping to dig for food, she returned home and went back to bed. Once again, she ate nothing and never stirred from where she lay. A few days later she visited the Deetkatoo again. By this time he was almost completely covered in the finest shells she had ever laid eyes upon.

By the seventh day her family realized that Mother possessed some very powerful magic and decided to leave her alone. Finally, after ten days, Mother got out of bed, washed and dressed, gathered up a large basket and went to the Deetkatoo. What a wonder he was to behold! The Deetkatoo looked like a doll all covered in seashells, mother-of-pearl, and fine bone. His head was made from a pair of finely carved buffalo-horn dishes. His eyes were fashioned from two smooth, shiny, oval beads the color of a summer sunset. Mother carefully plucked all the finery from the little fellow, piece by piece. When she was done, she returned home with her basketful of precious baubles.

Her family marveled at her newfound fortune. To her brothers she gave strings of spiral shell so long they hung to their waists. To her sisters-in-law she gave bead chokers that sparkled in the light. And for her children she made the fanciest headdresses and earrings in the land.

Upon hearing of this, Father paid a visit to his children. He was most curious as to how his son and daughter had obtained such finery. When Daughter told him that Mother had made everything, Father regretted that he had ever left his wife. So he returned home to his family and was a good husband and father from that day forward.

PIXIE

Mischief

PIXIES, WHO ARE ALSO KNOWN as piskies or pigsies, are found mostly in the southwestern counties of England. They bear some resemblance to brownies and other household fairies because they perform domestic chores for their favored mortals. They will vacate the premises permanently, however, if they are given new clothes by grateful mortals who are unaware that they are breaching fairy protocol.

Pixies vary in size; they are usually under three feet tall, but have been seen to appear as tall as mortals. No matter what their height may be, they are easily recognizable. Their clothes are green, their hair is red, their ears are pointed, and their noses turn up. Like most trooping fairies (fairies who band together), they dwell in large mounds, stone circles, and rock formations.

Pixies are some of the finest mischief-makers in the fairy realm. Some of their preferred sports include blowing out candles and leaving houses in the dark, pinching unsuspecting mortals, and riding horses at night until the poor beasts are exhausted and in a lather. But the particular brand of mischief for which they are best known is their game of leading travellers astray, a condition that is referred to as "pixie-led." It can be undone by wearing an article of clothing inside out.

Many fairy-friendly traits seem to be more appropriate in children than adults, and mischief is certainly one of them. Indeed, mischievous behavior in adults is usually perceived as childish, but that is usually because the pranks are harmful or not funny. Mischief, properly applied, can brighten a day or lighten the load of ordinary people laden with mundane burdens. Let your inner child come out to play, but just make sure your adult is there as chaperone.

The Pixie's Tale

WILLY AND NILLY WERE pixies who favored a home in Devon where two pretty serving girls worked. The girls were sometimes a little lazy, but it seldom mattered because Willy and Nilly did most of the work. In exchange for the pixies' services, the maidservants, Molly and Polly, left a silver coin for them every night in the chimney nook.

It so happened that one evening the girls forgot to leave a coin, which upset Willy and Nilly greatly. The pixie friends went up to the girls' room straightaway and protested loudly about their neglect. Polly was awakened by the fairies' boisterous complaining and nudged her friend Molly awake as well, to suggest that they go downstairs and make things right.

"I'll not move from this bed for all the pixies in Devonshire," yawned Molly, as she rolled over and went back to sleep. Polly sighed and went downstairs by herself to put a coin in the nook. Upon returning to the bedroom she overheard Willy and Nilly discussing what sort of vengeance they would wreak upon Molly. Polly's eyes grew wide with dread as she listened to the fairies' numerous schemes.

The pixies suggested withering her right hand so that she could no longer perform her duties, or making her mouth so foul and full of bitter fluid that no person would come near her again. After numerous ideas had been raised and rejected, the fairy friends agreed upon giving Molly a lame leg for seven years, after which time she could cure it with the application of a magical herb. The name of the herb was seven syllables long and impossible to pronounce. Poor Polly tried her best to retain all the details of the curse that was to befall her friend, but try as she might she could not remember the name of the healing herb.

The next morning Polly held her breath as she watched Molly rise from her bed. Sure enough, Molly's left leg was lame. Polly tried to console her friend with the news that her condition was only temporary, but seven years seemed like a lifetime to the youthful Molly. Molly's distress was aggravated even more when Polly found a small pile of silver coins that the pixies had left for her. Polly offered her lame companion half the amount left by the pixies, but Molly could not be comforted. No silver coin would restore her leg.

The years went by, more rapidly for Polly than Molly it seems. Polly had married a handsome stable boy and borne him two children, whereas Molly still worked as a serving girl. Poor Molly was really a good girl at heart and had learned her lesson well, for she never crossed the fairies again.

At last the seven years were done. Molly was glad that the term of her punishment was over but she despaired of ever finding the herb that could heal her, especially since she did not know its name.

Molly had adjusted to her physical affliction over the years, but she never grew accustomed to the loneliness that came with it. Though still young and bright, her lame leg did not make her good marriage material. One day, as she picked flowers in a sunlit meadow, with an eye open for a possible herb to heal her leg, she spied a strange-looking little boy playing in the grass. He looked very much like Willy and Nilly, although he was neither. All of a sudden, he struck hard at Molly's lame leg with a flowering herb he held in his hand. Molly felt her limb tingle and burn. When the strange sensations had ceased coursing through her calves, she began to walk; first one step, then another. And then another and another after that. Her limb had healed! She was no longer lame. Molly's joy knew no bounds. She began to dance about the meadow, laughing and crying all at the same time.

Molly recovered from the fairy mischief. Her happiness and gratitude made her shine like the morning sun. The young men who once rejected poor Molly because she was crippled now pursued her. But Molly was too busy for suitors. She practiced hard and became the finest, most graceful of dancers in the land, and that was the best thing of all.

MOUSE WOMAN

Balance

MOUSE WOMAN IS A DIMINUTIVE member of the supernatural world of the narnauks. Narnauks are spirits belonging to the folklore of the Northwest Coast Natives of Canada. They vary widely in size and are associated with animals, natural formations, and the elements of nature. Mouse Woman is a shapeshifter who sometimes appears as a small elderly woman, but her usual form is a mouselike fairy. When necessary, she can also make herself invisible.

There are a number of malicious narnauks, but Mouse Woman is not one of them. The worst she can be accused of is being nosy and interfering in other people's affairs. She also has the strange fetish for unraveling woolen articles with her tiny, spindly fingers. Her most beneficial compulsion is her need to redress imbalance and injustice, especially when the natural order of things has been upset.

Mouse Woman is a custodian of the delicate balance of nature in the fragile environment of the northwestern rainforests of North America. When the careless, selfish acts of mortals or evil narnauks threaten to destroy this perfect balance, Mouse Woman will intervene and use her supernatural abilities to restore it.

The most beautiful aspects of our world are consistently harmonious and whole, and yet mortals spend much of their time and energy destroying them. Mouse Woman is a magical creature capable of many wonders, but she cannot resolve all mortal transgressions. People do have the power to keep the magic of this beautiful planet alive themselves.

The Mouse Woman's Tale

Deep in the mountain forests there once lived an evil narnauk named Snee-Nee-Iq who stole children from their homes and ate them. This distressed Mouse Woman greatly, for she was a good narnauk and took much pleasure in setting bad things right.

One hot summer night, a very spoiled little girl, who lived in the village at the foot of the mountain where Snee-Nee-Iq dwelt, wanted some goat's tallow as a treat. Everyone had finished eating and had gone to bed, so the girl's mother refused to concede to her daughter's demands. The troublesome girl began to wail so loudly that the entire village was kept awake by her bellowing. Her mother threatened to turn her out of doors if she did not cease her caterwauling, so that she would fall prey to Snee-Nee-Iq. This had little effect on the girl because she did not believe in Snee-Nee-Iq.

Although she screamed incessantly, the little girl managed to discern the eerie sound of a voice in the wind as it howled outside. The voice told the little girl that it would give her the delicacy she desired. The little girl ran out of the house seeking the source of the disembodied voice. She had barely stepped out the door when she spied a giant woman standing head and shoulders above a grove of trees not far from the village. The giant gestured to the young girl to follow her.

"Come with me and you will get your goat's tallow," said Snee-Nee-Iq.

Still believing that the giant would not harm her, the girl followed, her mouth watering in anticipation of the snack that awaited her. Soon the little girl tired of climbing up the steep slope and began to complain vociferously. The giant swept the girl up in her massive arms, plonked her into a basket on her back, and carried her the rest of the way.

"Where's my goat's tallow?" demanded the little girl, as soon as she was dumped on the floor of Snee-Nee-Iq's hut.

"First you must eat some ripe, red berries," replied the giant. And out she went to pick them. The little girl lay down to wait. As she began to nod off, she felt something tug at her clothes. When she opened her eyes she saw a tiny grandmother, no bigger than a mouse, sitting on her stomach.

"Don't eat the berries of Snee-Nee-Iq, my dear," warned Mouse Woman. "If you eat the berries, you will fall under her spell and then she will eat you." Before the little girl had a chance to respond, Mouse Woman asked the little girl for her woolen hair ornaments.

"Throw them in the fire as an offering," Mouse Woman told her. The little girl did as the narnauk asked. The ornaments had barely landed on the fire when Mouse Woman snatched them out of the flames and began unraveling them until only a pile of brightly colored yarn remained. Then the little grandmother vanished.

When Snee-Nee-Iq finally returned with a basketful of berries, the little girl refused to eat them unless she had some goat's tallow first. Off went Snee-Nee-Iq to get some goat's tallow, grumbling all the way. As soon as the giant was out of the door, the mousy narnauk reappeared.

"Do not eat the goat's tallow Snee-Nee-Iq offers you. It is really the fat of human flesh," Mouse Woman said solemnly. Then she gave the little girl elaborate instructions on how to defeat Snee-Nee-Iq. She made the girl fetch ten black mountain goat horns, which were hidden in the corner of the hut, and put one horn on each of her fingers. Then the little grandmother taught the girl a magic spell.

When the two conspirators spied Snee-Nee-Iq coming back up the mountain, the girl pointed her horny fingers at the giant and repeated the spell three times. Nothing happened. When the girl said the spell a fourth time, the giant fell backward and tumbled down the mountain slope. When she came to a halt at the bottom of the mountain, Mouse Woman shoved a flaming torch in the little girl's hand and instructed her to set the giant on fire. The terrified child did as she was told and the giant burst into flames. Each of the glowing ashes that rose from the burning giant turned into a ravenous mosquito. The angry horde of blood-sucking insects turned on the little girl and chased her all the way back to her village.

The mosquitoes she brought back with her reaffirmed her place as the most unpopular citizen in the village. But Mouse Woman was pleased, for that was all part of the balance in a just and ordered world.

MORGAN LE FAY

Glamour

THERE HAS BEEN CONSIDERABLE controversy about the fairy status of Morgan le Fay. In her most human incarnation she has been depicted as a powerful enchantress and evil half-sister of King Arthur of Camelot. As the Arthurian version of Morrigan, the Celtic triple goddess, she acquires divine proportions. It is the accounts of her childhood on the fairy isle of Avalon, however, where she was educated in the Old Ways and the arts of necromancy, that indicate the fairy blood running in her veins. Her uncertain genealogy is perhaps the surest sign of her Otherworldly origins.

The best-known stories of her life are found in the Arthurian romances, where she is portrayed as the enemy of Arthur and Guinevere. Most accounts of the Arthurian legend reflect Christian sensibilities, which is why Morgan received such bad press. Morgan le Fay was a staunch defender of the fairy faith when Christianity was encroaching upon pagan Britain.

Morgan le Fay possessed many magical powers, not the least of which was glamour. "Glamour" is an old Scottish word that describes the spell cast by fairies and witches to alter the appearance of reality. Glamour makes something appear other than it really is.

Fairy glamour is powerful magic. But, for all its glamour, it is fleeting and illusory. There are many mortals whose outwardly glamorous lives are only the thinnest of veneers, masking their less-than-ideal private lives. The power of glamour is a useful thing to have if a mortal remains aware that its effect is only temporary. All illusion has a price.

Morgan Le Fay's Tale

ORGAN LE FAY'S HEART had been broken by the death of her lover, Accolon of Gaul, at the hands of her half-brother, Arthur, King of Britain. Arthur had entrusted her with the mighty sword Excalibur, but Morgan gave it to her paramour, Accolon, so that he could use it against the King. In a contest between champions, Arthur, using an ordinary sword that had been magically fashioned by Morgan to appear in the likeness of Excalibur, commenced battle with Accolon. Accolon had just taken the upper hand when suddenly the Lady of the Lake appeared and warned Arthur of Morgan's deception. The Lady of the Lake enchanted Excalibur so that Arthur could seize the great sword from Accolon and slay him.

Morgan was stricken with grief. There was no part of her deepest self that was safe from Arthur. Once again she plotted to render Arthur incapable of destroying her and the way of life she, her sisters, and brothers in faith had known. Morgan hastened to the convent where Arthur was recovering from his battle with Accolon. She stole into his chambers while he slept and took from his bedside a magnificent scabbard, made of gold and precious jewels. Morgan knew that so long as Arthur wore the charmed scabbard he would not shed blood. She hid it beneath her robes and escaped from the abbey under the guise of night.

Upon waking and discovering that his precious scabbard was gone, Arthur knew at once that the enchantress Morgan had paid him a visit while he was sleeping. Arthur quickly assembled his horses and men and set out over the countryside in pursuit of Morgan. When Morgan ascertained that Arthur and his forces were gaining upon her party, she threw the scabbard deep into a nearby lake. Morgan had no power against the king when he was protected by the Lady of the Lake, who was close at hand. As she heard the thundering hooves of Arthur and his men approaching, Morgan stretched her arms upward and brought in a bitterly cold wind that whipped around her women and horses—all were frozen in their place. A moment later, when the wind had ceased its fury, a ring of stones stood where Morgan and her party had been only moments before.

Arthur arrived moments later at the ominous stone circle. As he looked intently at each the stones, he could discern the features of every woman and animal clearly. Encased in her marble shell, Morgan looked even more forbidding than she did in life. He left shortly, in stunned silence. When Arthur and his knights had disappeared from sight, Morgan resumed her normal human shape.

The next day Morgan despatched one of her knights to Arthur at Camelot bearing a message from her. It was a warning and a declaration: "I will never fear you so long as I have the power to change my shape into stone."

After this taunting message between sister and brother, the two fell silent for several months. But Morgan had not ceased plotting against Arthur. She made a crimson cloak decorated with delicate gold and silver thread and embroidered with the finest, most radiant gemstones of emerald, sapphire, and ruby —and into the cloak she wove a spell that only death of the wearer could unbind.

When at last the leaves had fallen from the trees and the chill winds of winter ripped across the snowcovered plains, Morgan sent a maiden messenger to Arthur with the splendid cloak as a gift of peace. Once again the Lady of the Lake appeared to Arthur and advised him not to wear the cloak that Morgan offered him. So Arthur instructed the handmaiden who had brought the cloak to put it on herself. The girl protested and said it would not be seemly for such a one as herself to wear a cloak befitting a King. But Arthur insisted, for it was a cloak worthy of a better look. The maiden obeyed her King by spreading the great robe across her slender shoulders. As she stood engulfed in the voluminous folds of the wondrous garment, she began to tremble fiercely, and then burst into flames before the whole assembly.

Arthur and the court watched in horror as the hapless maiden was consumed by fire. Moments later nothing remained of her but smoldering ashes. The maiden had paid for her loyalty to mistress and king with her life.

NORNS

Fate

THE THREE SCANDINAVIAN SISTERS of fate, the Norns, are named Urd, Verdandi, and Skuld, and represent past, present, and future respectively. They are traditionally known to appear at the birth of noble personages, bestow a gift or a curse, and foretell the fate of the child. In some versions of *Sleeping Beauty*, seven or thirteen fairies of fate turn up at the christening of the princess to offer their blessings.

It is hard to imagine how the arrival of thirteen sisters of fate could not be received without some apprehension, for they are known for their macabre beauty. Norns have long, thin bodies draped in gray robes, and wear veils over their heads to soften their penetrating vision.

The Weird Sisters of Shakespeare's *Macbeth* are the Saxon variant of the Norns. ("Weird" is derived from the Old English word *wyrd*, meaning fate.) Despite the dire warnings and predictions of the witches, Macbeth always had choices. His fate was sealed by his own hand.

Most mortals feel that the Norns are ominous. They weave the patterns of people's lives, but the threads that hold the web together are gossamer fine. A person can choose to break those threads completely, or reinforce them, as need be. The Norns do not deny any mortal the opportunity to play a hand in their own existence and to take charge of their own destiny.

People who allow themselves to get caught in self-defeating patterns can lose control of their lives and become the helpless victims of fate. Everyone has a choice. Take ownership of your actions and learn when to surrender. Be the master or mistress of your own fate.

The Norns' Tale

MY NAME IS URD. I am the eldest of three sisters who are fated to be forever entangled in the earthly affairs of mortals. My second sister is Verdandi, who rules the present. The youngest is Skuld, who knows the future. My place is in the past, where I replenish the well of remembrance with the stories of humankind. The stories are retold again and again, but still there are mortals who do not listen. My sisters and I once knew such as man as that, and his name was Macbeth.

Macbeth was born of noble lineage and was graced with more than most men. But he was destined to undo his gifts because he was not satisfied with his lot, for he lusted after Scotland's crown. My sisters and I knew of his vaulting ambition, so we helped him weave the strands of his life in accordance with his birthright—no more and no less.

We wore the guise of witches when we spoke to him, and warned him where his path might lead. We hailed him as Thane of Cawdor and King of the Realm before he had ever achieved these ranks. For this he was more puzzled than pleased. He questioned our motives, whether for good or ill, but chose not to find an answer for himself. We told him only of what might be when ambition is everything and justice and right make no account.

We sent phantasms to him that bore no good, yet he played fortune's fool and did not make a stand. For his sake we showed him the fatal vision of a bloody dagger moments before he set his plan in motion. Despite his fear and doubt, he followed the dagger straight to King Duncan's chamber where he murdered the monarch in his sleep. Surely it was a sign that bode ill, and still he blamed us for leading him on. When he murdered again, twice over, my youngest sister cried out to him that he would sleep no more. What else does any man need to know of his fate?

Hecate, Queen of the Crossroads and Mistress of Magic, chastised my sisters and me for wasting our efforts on such a wayward son. Macbeth did not respect us. He spurned fate and pursued his own ends against all wisdom and despite all fear.

The Queen of the Crossroads looked on as we prepared to summon his future out of our caldron, where all time is now. Macbeth arrived, as we knew he would, and asked us what we were doing. "A deed without a name," we replied together. It was for Macbeth to name the deed, because it was his fate we invoked. But he named neither his thoughts false nor his deeds wicked. It was easier to blame us than account for himself.

The visions we conjured spoke in riddles and rhymes, which confused him more, but discouraged him not. The fateful specters that appeared from the caldron warned Macbeth of his enemies and of the circumstances that would bring him down. No man born of a woman would harm him, the visions foretold. Nor should he fear death until the woods of Birnam came to Dunsinane hill. And still he asked to see more.

We conjured one more vision, the one he feared most. Before him appeared a line of eight kings. Then came Banquo, whom he had murdered. It would be Banquo, we had first told Macbeth, who would lead a succession of kings, though he would ne'er be one himself. At this dreaded sight Macbeth scorned us and reviled our good work. He did not seek our counsel again, nor would we have given

it. We had only to wait and watch his sorry tale unfold. Our work with Macbeth was ended, though his had not begun, and never would. Not once did he pick up the threads of his own fate. The bloody fabric we wove was Macbeth's undoing, 'tis true. But he chose to wear a garment he did not own and paid dearly for it.

In the final battle for the crown, his enemies wore the branches of Birnam Forest to approach Dunsinane castle by stealth, where Macbeth awaited his fate. Despite the evidence before him, Macbeth was unmoved from his course. Thus was he defeated by his enemy Macduff, who was taken from his mother's womb while still inside the sac that kept him warm. Upon learning the truth about the man who would take his life, Macbeth finally heeded the words of my sisters and me. He cursed us aloud and refused to fight a battle he could not win. But his cowardly action was too late. The last thread that remained was too fragile to repair the sticky web that had engulfed him and finally destroyed him.

My name is Urd and I am the eldest of three sisters who rule past and present and future. We are fated to be forever entangled in the affairs and lives of mortal men.

FAMILIAR
Service

A FAMILIAR IS AN ELEMENTAL WHO takes the form of an inanimate object or, more frequently, an animal companion. The term is derived from the Latin word *famulus*, meaning servant. Familiars are found in numerous cultures throughout the world: Australian Aborigines, South African Zulus, Native North Americans, and peoples of southeast Asia have all used the help of familiars in their spiritual and psychic practices.

In Europe, familiars are most commonly known to serve witches in the form of a cat, but toads and rabbits are frequently associated with wise women as well. Familiars are a physical connection to the psychic realm, offering protection and guidance to their human partners in the exploration of Otherworlds.

Being in a position of service does not denote servitude. It is a deeply humbling, ennobling experience. To genuinely serve another is to put that person's interest before your own. It is to defer to another; to offer them esteem. When people are thus honored, they are inclined to behave in a manner deserving of such respect. A person who is weak or unsure of themselves or their own power cannot have humility. Real humility is demonstrated by people who are completely at peace with themselves and their place in the world.

The Familiar's Tale

MY MISTRESS IS A DREAMER and a wordsmith by trade. If she could make a living from her dreams she would be wealthy beyond the wildest of them. During the day she dreams about her hopes; at night it is her fears. It is my role in life to guide her through the murky depths of her mind and help her face the monsters that lurk there. I am her feline companion and servant. In exchange for my invaluable services, she grooms me a little, feeds me enough, and loves me too much. I tolerate her numerous human weaknesses because she is a basically good mortal and has a rich inner life, to which I am privy. For centuries I have appeared in many guises and served many generations of mortals, and I am pleased to say that my present mistress's interior landscape measures up to the best of them. She keeps me on my paws. (Please forgive the feline cliché. I do not share my mistress's facility with words.)

My mistress, whose name is Fay, spends much of her time in dreamland, which is only one of its many names. Some of Fay's friends think that the sad and lonely dreamscape where she spends most of her time is an escape from reality and therefore detrimental to her well-being. What fools these mortals be. They do not see the truth of dreams. The world where she spends her best time is not an escape from reality, it is the exploration of another reality.

There was a time, not so long ago, when my mistress had more than the usual number of reasons to retreat into my world. Fay's dreams of success and fulfilment were always thwarted by forces she could not name. So one night, as she dreamed, I went with her. I followed her to a land far away and long ago, where she walked down a cobblestone street in a quaint, fairy-tale town. Fay walked for a long while, frequently stopping and peering through the shop windows that lined the narrow street. At last she stopped in front of a shop with a sign that read "World's Only Printing Press." Fay walked in and I followed. A very large, old printing press dominated the tiny shop. A dark, forbidding woman stood in front of the press, blocking my mistress's way.

"The printing press is out of order," said the woman. "You'll have to go elsewhere."

I expressed my extreme aversion for the wicked woman with some impressive hissing and a display of my teeth.

"Oh, what's the use?" my mistress sighed. "She won't start the press."

Fay awoke when her sobs made it hard for her to breathe. As a counterpoint to that sad sight, I padded, ever so gently, all over her pillow, rubbing against her moist cheeks and purring deliciously.

Sometimes my mistress is slow in learning her lessons. I really had had enough of her sad dreams and decided to take matters into my own paws. The very next night I took my mistress on a journey into the sleeping mind of the dark woman of the printing press.

I led my mistress down a long, dimly lit corridor. We walked for such a long time that Fay began to complain about the oppressive atmosphere of her dream.

"This is not your dream," I told her. "You are just a visitor here."

We reached the end of the hallway at last, where an oak door barred the rest of the way. I commanded Fay to open it, which she did, very gingerly. The door opened into a bare, gray, windowless room. In the center of the room stood the dark woman.

"Fancy meeting you here," she snarled.

"Yes, fancy that," my mistress answered, producing a pen from her breast pocket and pointing it at the enemy.

"Take that, and that, and that!" she crowed, waving her pen triumphantly. The pen spewed a thick, black stream of ink all over the dark woman. Fay brandished her magic pen, crossing t's and dotting i's on the woman's bodice, where it burned like acid right through to her flesh. That is when the dark woman woke up screaming.

My mistress's circumstances have improved of late. She writes about her dreams as much as she lives in them. She does not remember her appearance in the other woman's dream, however. She cannot recall the journey we took together to start the wheel of fortune turning. But I keep that memory for her, and many more besides, because that is what I do.

HU HSIEN

Guile

THERE ARE HUNDREDS OF folktales in China and Japan about the Hu Hsien, also known as fox fairies. Like most fairies, they elude precise description because they are neither completely good nor totally bad. Certain characteristics, however, emerge from the vast store of tales that have been told and written about them.

Fox fairies are excellent shapeshifters, usually transforming themselves into old men, scholars, or beautiful maidens, although they have been known to appear to mortals in their fox shape. They are typically predisposed to trickery, sometimes just for fun and at other times out of sheer malice. Whether they are intentionally cruel or not, they take great delight in cunning deception, testing mortals for their wit and their virtue.

Guile is certainly one of the more unpleasant features encountered in Otherworld spirits, at least by mortal standards. It leads to mistrust and scepticism, feelings that do not render a person open to magic. Caution, rather than suspicion, should always be practiced in the fairy realm, where there is deception for the unwary mortal at every turn, often in the most appealing and seductive of guises. This can be very hard to resist.

The mortal realm has more than its share of untrustworthy denizens as well. There is considerable wisdom in the adage "too good to be true." Unlike charm or glamour, guile is almost always a mask for something unpleasant or dishonest. The Hu Hsien teach us to exercise caution when something seems better than what is expected, especially in unfamiliar circumstances. Always scratch a polished surface to find the truth that lies beneath.

The Hu Hsien's Tale

MA TIEN-JUNG WAS A poor Chinese peasant who had lost his wife when he was only twenty years old. If he had been of noble birth or even a prosperous farmer, he would have arranged for a second wife, but circumstances dictated that he remain impoverished and alone.

Ma was tilling the fields one day when he noticed a fair young woman walking across the fields directly toward him. Her aristocratic bearing and fine clothes were so out of keeping with her surroundings that Ma assumed she had lost her way and was approaching him for directions. Despite the obvious differences in their station, Ma began to flirt outrageously with the young woman, and she responded with a promise to visit him later that night.

Ma was certain that the girl was teasing him, so he was all the more delighted when she appeared on his doorstep at the stroke of midnight. Ma looked at the maiden standing at the door and in the soft glow of the moon he could discern that her body was covered in fine, reddish hair. He knew at once that this mysterious young woman must be a fox fairy.

"If you are truly one of those fantastic creatures, then perhaps you can help me out with a little money to see me through lean times," he suggested, as demurely as his coarse breeding would allow.

After a passionate night with the farmer, the lovely maid left in the morning with the promise that she would be happy to help ease his poverty. She returned again that very night, and when Ma asked her for the money, she seemed genuinely distressed that she had forgotten to bring it. After another night of bliss, the foxy maid assured him that she would return with the money. But she forgot the money again when she paid Ma a third visit.

The pretty maid continued to visit the farmer every night for several weeks until, finally, after Ma had given up asking her, she produced two silver coins. Poverty had taught Ma lessons in frugality, so he stored the coins away for the future. A few months later, while paying a merchant for farming utensils, he was shocked to discover that they weren't silver at all but pewter. That evening Ma admonished his fairy lover for her deception.

"I simply paid you according to your worth," she told him. "You are a lowly peasant and not worth much."

Offended by her snobbery, Ma tried to repay her in kind. "Fox fairies are supposed to be creatures of uncommon beauty. Why aren't you?" he taunted.

The fox fairy replied that she had taken her present form according to his station. Her appearance, she said, was sufficiently attractive for the likes of him.

The fox fairy did not visit Ma for several months. Ma had finally stopped pining for her when she returned again. Before speaking, the fox fairy presented him with three silver coins.

"Until now I have refrained from giving you money due to your humble circumstances," the fox fairy said, "but now that you're getting married I will give you enough coins to pay for bride-money. It is my parting gift to you."

When Ma told her he was not engaged, she informed him that a matchmaker would be contacting him shortly. Still doubtful, Ma begged the fairy to tell him what his new bride-to-be would look like.

"Just as you wanted her to look. She will possess uncommon attractiveness," responded the fox fairy.

The next day Ma was visited by a matchmaker. Unsure of the fox fairy's designs, Ma asked to see the girl before he agreed to marry her.

It was the custom in those days that respectable girls did not allow themselves to be seen by their future husbands before the nuptials. So the matchmaker arranged for Ma to sneak a peek at his bride-to-be. The young girl lived in the same house as a relative of the matchmaker, which provided a good excuse for them to visit the court and observe the girl unnoticed. As they walked through the hall of the court, Ma saw his intended sitting down in a chair, her head bent forward, while an attendant leaned over her, scratching her back. From where Ma stood the girl appeared to be just as the matchmaker had described her.

The final arrangements for the wedding were made, the matchmaker's fee and bride-money was paid, and on the appointed day Ma's fiancée came to his house. Ma gasped when he opened the door. Her head was bent over, half way down her breast, just as he had first seen her. Unfortunately, that was the way she would always remain, because she was humpbacked.

Ma sighed in resignation as he remembered the final words of his foxy lover.

DRYAD
Growth

DRYADS ARE WOOD NYMPHS whose folklore originated in ancient Greece, although similar types of forest spirits are an age-old global phenomenon. Dryads are tree-dwellers, but may leave their host tree and roam about the forest freely. Hamadryads are tree nymphs, embodied by the tree that houses them, which is most frequently the oak. They prosper and grow in accord with the life of their host, protecting their woody abode just as if it were their own flesh and blood.

Dryads are lovely and lithe with long, green hair. The forms of the tree-bound hamadryads emerge upward out of the trunk, so that only their upper half resembles a human body. Both types of spirits are usually benign but they will retaliate if there is an assault upon their natural environment.

The inability of many mortals to recognize the life force—that which is beneath the surface of all living things—results in a mundane existence. Unfortunately, deliberate disregard for this essence can be dangerous and more far-reaching, leading to death and extinction. Life force is manifested in myriad forms in the people, places, and things all around us; it is the essence that has been a part of everything since the world was born.

At the very least, a mortal can feel spirits, which is why forests are a place of mystery and magic to sensitive individuals, and not something to exploit. Being able to recognize that which is unseen is not superstition, it is respect for the spirit that exists within everything that lives and grows.

The Dryad's Tale

I STAND ALONE NOW ON the ancient land of my home. There was a time, not so long ago, when I and many thousands of my sisters lived on this once great land together. My family was a magnificent forest of oak and cedar, pine and birch. My sisters and I had many children, who have all now gone. They were the birds and beasts who lived in our branches, ate our fruit, and spread our seeds.

Hordes of these creatures struggled daily for their lives. They rejoiced and grieved, played and fought, fed and starved, lived and died, in numbers too great to count, over time too long to measure. I watched their awesome toil for two hundred full turns of the seasons, and then there was nothing. But I stand here and remember. I stand as a sentinel to the memory of the lost creatures of this land, and to my own ancestors whose vital juices still flow in my veins.

I once had a name, but have no need for it now. For there is no one or nothing to remember me. All living forms that could move did so—far away, I know not where. They ran and flew, crawled and burrowed, slithered and swam away from here, despite the pleas of my remaining sisters and me. Perhaps they think that we betrayed them, but that is not so.

My sisters were sacrificed to mighty beasts so hard and unbending we could not withstand them. They lumbered and roared among us, tearing us down with their shiny claws and their thundering blows. Those monsters, so hard, so resistant, and without any soul, felled us by the thousands, day after day, season upon season, until there were no more. Save me alone. But I am not done. Oh no, not yet.

I am proud of my sisters, for they did not go down without a fight. You may well wonder how we, who cannot move from where we stand, and must bend or break to unconscionable tyranny, can oppose such a fierce enemy. It is because we have power of place. We stand our ground. You may laugh and say we have no choice, but you are wrong.

One by one, as my sisters fell, I heard them scream in pain and fear. I heard them rail against the fates, and I heard them beg for their lives. But those horrid, rolling monsters aided by all those false, sharp tongues with their hundreds of tiny teeth were deaf to my sisters' pleas. Perhaps they could not hear over the calamitous clamor of their grumbling war cries. No sound of the forest could match such a dreadful din; not the roar of lion or bear, nor the thunder of water falling over a chasm. The only sounds more dreadful were the last cries of my sisters as they fell to the ground. And what cries of portent they were. All the animals, birds, and insects of the forest heard and understood, so did all the waters, still and flowing, as did the flowers and grasses that lay at our feet. For the final cries of all my sister spirits were curses, deep and dark.

"A curse on thee and all your kind," they cried. "Cursed be your children, and cursed be your homes. May the darkness you create come and swallow you whole." My sisters' hexes made my leaves tremble and fall. No wind could shake me as those words did that echoed across the land.

The rampage continued for so many seasons that I dared count them no longer. Finally, the rolling monsters dragged away the last of the empty, lifeless shells of my sisters. Silence fell at last upon the barren land. But it was not the full, serene silence I had known before the enemy came. How different is the stillness of death from the stillness that exists when all nature breathes and sings, when life bursts forth and then passes away in its proper time. There was daily life-and-death chaos and commotion in my forest home but, for all that, it was a quiet, peaceful place. This was the wonder and magic of my forest home, but it has gone away forever, as I must, too.

The spirits of wind and rain have not ceased their mourning. The winds howl their rage, the lakes and rivers overflow and flood the land with their tears. Then the droughts come and the sun burns the despoiled earth. Nothing grows, nothing lives. Together, my sisters and I were once able to protect the land from some of nature's wrath. But I am alone now. My sisters' curses have come to pass. There is no magic that can undo our fate and save our world.

Now I die, too, for my time has come.
I am the last tree.
Who will remember me?

UGUNSMATE

Home

I N LATVIA, UGUNSMATE IS THE female guardian spirit of the hearth. Many of the most significant elements of Latvian rural life are protected by maternal spirits. (*Mate* is Latvian for mother.) Ugunsmate is a central figure in the domestic life of rural homes and families, and important to their physical and spiritual well-being.

Like most beings of the Latvian spirit world, Ugunsmate very seldom appears in corporeal form. Her presence is usually noted by a strong sense of place and communal good feeling, even when her custodial fire does not burn. Her absence is easily detected by discord, misfortune, and mishap.

On the few occasions she has been seen in human form, Ugunsmate appears as a kind, maternal figure dressed in a fiery red and gold national costume. On her head she wears a radiant, scarlet headdress. She has been reported, however, to appear in a more ethereal, ephemeral state amid the smoke and flames of the hearth.

The hearth is the heart of a home. Before the advent of central heating, the hearth provided heat, light, and a means for cooking food. It was central to the smooth running of daily domestic affairs and special family gatherings, when stories were told and songs were sung. Ugunsmate teaches us the importance of home; a place to feel grounded and safe.

When mortals who have ventured into the Otherworld return to this realm, they frequently feel restless, uprooted, and harbor a profound longing to "go home." Home is not necessarily a physical place. It is built on a foundation of love. Follow your bliss. Wherever the fires of the heart burn with passion and commitment, there you will find your true home.

Ugunsmate's Tale

IN A LAND FAR AWAY and long ago there lived a little girl named Maija. In the summer she would run in the fields and meadows of her homeland, chasing butterflies and picking daisies to make flower wreaths to crown her head. When winter came she made angels in the snow and built castles of ice with her friends. But most of all she loved to sit by the hearth and listen to her mother tell stories. Sometimes her mother told tales of when she was a little girl, and how she tended the fire and waited for Ugunsmate to appear to her in her fairy form.

Ugunsmate looked after those who tended the hearth. As long as the home fires burned, Ugunsmate would protect and provide for the family. Imagine the great sense of responsibility that Maija felt when one day her mother passed this duty on to her.

Maija learned how to stack the kindling, stoke the embers, and fan the flames to keep the fire burning. She was never frightened by the flames because she knew that Ugunsmate would protect her. As Maija grew older, she became bolder and more reckless with her duties because she was certain that Ugunsmate would look after her, no matter how she tempted fate. She believed that if she could make the fire big enough, Ugunsmate would reveal herself.

"What does Ugunsmate look like?" she asked her mother frequently.

Her mother's reply was always the same. "Magic," her mother said, "Ugunsmate looks like magic."

Maija was never the wiser for this answer, because she didn't know what magic looked like, if it looked like anything at all.

Maija never tired of staring into the fire for hours, looking for Ugunsmate. One day she announced to her mother that the sparks shooting out of the burning logs and drifting up the chimney were fire fairies who longed to be free of the confines of the hearth.

"That's right," her mother agreed, "they are the children of Ugunsmate. When they are ready to leave the safety of the hearth they go out and search for a home to call their own. Such is the way of all children." Maija didn't want to believe her mother's words. She never wanted to leave her childhood home.

But that is exactly what came to pass. Maija grew up and found a home of her own with a husband she loved with all her heart and soul and a daughter she loved even more. Maija taught her daughter all the things that her mother had taught her, especially how to tend the fire. One day her daughter asked her if she had ever seen Ugunsmate. "No," was Maija's sad reply.

Grown-up Maija had a lovely home and hearth of her own, but she missed her mother's stories. So every Sunday Maija and her new family would visit her mother. After a scrumptious Sunday dinner, everyone gathered around the hearth and listened to her mother weave tales of wonder and magic. Try as she might, Maija was never able to tell a story in the same captivating way her mother did.

One day the fire stopped burning in the hearth of Maija's house. Her mother had died. She had lived a long time and had a good life, but Maija was stricken with grief nonetheless. For a while the flame in Maija's heart died too.

"Don't cry, Mama," her daughter consoled her as she sat by the hearth and wept, "I know how to light a fire. I can take care of the hearth, so don't you worry."

Maija kissed her daughter and went to bed. She was angry with Ugunsmate for abandoning her when she needed her most. Maybe her daughter would be able to start the fire.

Maija's daughter had learned her lessons well. She loved to build the fire high and stare into it just as Maija had done as a child. From where she lay in bed, Maija could hear her daughter stacking the wood, and soon she could hear that her daughter had succeeded in bringing the hearth back to life. Maija nodded off to sleep listening to the spit and crackle of the flames.

Maija was deeply asleep when she was suddenly awakened by her daughter's excited cries. She jumped out of bed and ran to the hearth to see what all the commotion was about. It seemed to her that the flames in the hearth had never burned brighter.

"Mama, Mama!" her daughter clamored, "I saw her. I saw Ugunsmate. I saw her in the fire! And guess what, Mama? Ugunsmate looks just like Grandma."

NINGYO

Bliss

HE NINGYO ARE THE MERFOLK of Japanese folklore and legend and share many of the characteristics of water spirits everywhere. Like the sea in which they dwell, they can be beautiful and serene, or fierce and treacherous. Ningyo are reported to have human upper bodies, but fish tails from the waist down, just like the merfolk of occidental myth. However, in most accounts they are dressed in long, brightly colored silk gowns, which waft gracefully behind them as they move about their watery homes, concealing whatever lies underneath. They live luxuriously in glorious palaces at the bottom of the ocean, and will spend hours floating weightlessly through magnificent halls and splendid gardens, simply for the sheer pleasure of it.

Like many water-dwelling fairies around the world, the Ningyo can be very seductive spirits, offering mortals a life of physical and spiritual bliss. Many mortals who enter into the fairy realm experience a rapture that is unparalleled in this world. Such an idyllic life does not always come without exacting a high price, however. Like a good wine, the intoxicating effects of blissful existence can render a person forgetful and irresponsible.

When mortals encounter Otherworldly bliss, they lose all sense of time—especially if they have partaken of any fairy food or drink—and eventually suffer for abandoning their worldly responsibilities, however inadvertently. Ordinary reality very quickly reveals the temporal nature of bliss. Bliss is a rewarding and delightful consequence derived from specific thoughts and deeds and is not a permanent state; at least, not in this world.

The Ningyo's Tale

URASHIMA TARO WAS A young man and the finest fisherman in the little village where he lived. He was descended from a long line of fishermen, and upheld his humble station in life with the dignity and honor befitting of a nobleman.

One lovely summer's evening, as he was walking home from a day of fishing, he spied a group of young boys mistreating a turtle. The boys laughed cruelly as they beat the poor creature with sticks and stones. Urashima felt compassion for the innocent animal and reprimanded the children for their heartless behavior. But the boys paid no heed, for they were simply acting in a way that immature, young people sometimes do when they are bored.

It was clear to Urashima that the boys had no intention of ending their cruel game, so he offered to buy the hapless turtle from them. The boys accepted Urashima's money and quickly ran away, leaving Urashima alone with the turtle. He picked up the poor, put-upon creature and carried it to the seashore. After he had laid the turtle in the shallows, Urashima waited and watched until it swam safely out to sea and disappeared over the horizon.

The next morning, as he sat in his fishing boat waiting for his nets to fill, his mind turned to the turtle he had saved the day before. How nice to be a turtle, as they live for so long, he pondered. While his thoughts were thus engaged he heard a voice calling his name. He peered over the side of the boat in the direction of the voice and saw the turtle he had rescued. The turtle thanked Urashima for his kindness and asked him if he had ever visited the palace of the Dragon King of the Sea. Urashima replied that the Dragon King's palace was only a legend and not a real place at all, although if indeed there were such a splendid palace, he would enjoy seeing it very much.

"Hop on my back and I will take you there," said the turtle. No sooner were the words out of the turtle's mouth when it grew to four times its original size. Although stupefied with wonder, Urashima managed to climb onto the turtle's back. Down went the two companions into the sea, far away and deeper and deeper, until at last Urashima saw a magnificent palace made from mother-of-pearl and coral, shimmering beautifully through the translucent sea waters.

Urashima and the turtle were met with great pomp and circumstance at the palace gates by attendant fish that glowed bright yellow and blue. Urashima followed the fishy servants to a great hall where he beheld the loveliest lady he had ever seen. She wore an exquisite green gown that wafted gracefully all around her.

"Welcome to my father's palace," said the Sea Princess. "I was the turtle whose life you saved. For your kindness you may stay here with me and live in beauty and splendor for the rest of your life." Instantly overwhelmed with love for the princess, Urashima agreed without hesitation.

For three days and nights Urashima and the lovely Sea Princess lived together in complete and utter bliss. The Sea Princess showed Urashima all the delights and wonders of his new home. Never had he seen such elegance and grandeur. Most beautiful of all was the palace garden, where fish, birds, and insects lived together amid a sea of flowers and trees.

On the fourth day, Urashima suddenly remembered his elderly parents back home. "I must return to my parents to tell them what has become of me," he told the princess. When he could not be persuaded to stay, the princess gave Urashima a finely lacquered box, with a warning that he must never open it.

Urashima left the sea palace the same way he had arrived, on the back of a turtle. As soon as he stepped on the shores of his childhood home, he was filled with foreboding. The mountains and forests were the same but the village had changed. There were strange new houses and faces wherever he turned.

"My name is Urashima Taro and I am looking for my parents," he said to the first stranger he encountered. Imagine the shock he felt when the stranger told him that a man named Urashima Taro had lived in the village three hundred years before. He had gone fishing one day and never returned. His parents, of course, were long dead.

Urashima returned to the beach with the wooden box. Despite the princess's warning, and although he was grieving for the loss of his parents, simple human curiosity spurred him on to open it. No sooner had he lifted the lid when a thin, sinuous wisp of purple vapor floated out of the box. While Urashima was gazing in wonder at the magical mist, his skin began to crinkle like old paper. Moments later nothing remained of Urashima Taro but a pile of dust.

BROWNIE

Order

ROWNIES ARE BENIGN MALE FAIRIES (although a few females have been reported) who can be found throughout Britain. Usually no more than three feet high, some have been noted to wear brown, shabby clothes, some are clad in green, and still others appear to be sporting nothing but a shaggy coat of hair. Some variations of this peculiar fairy depict him with only two holes in his face for a nose. The brownie is a solitary sprite who frequently attaches himself to a particular household or person. Any sort of lavish payment for the domestic help he provides around the house or farm, such as cleaning dishes or reaping hay, is offensive to him and causes him to vanish forever. He will, however, gladly accept a bowl of milk or cream for his services.

To enjoy the services of a brownie, a mortal must follow a very strict code of behavior. The brownie will maintain order in his own portion of this world, which he shares with his mortal companions, as long as they show respect for brownie protocol. Any breach of protocol destroys the order that the brownie has worked hard to preserve, and it is almost always the human who has the most to lose. The brownie shows ordinary people that an ordered existence is not necessarily rigid or mundane. In fact, a little order in one's life can be just the key to open the portals to the fairy realm. Order clears the heart and mind, leaving room for magic to bloom and grow when the time is right.

The Brownie's Tale

THERE WAS NEVER A MORE loyal, hardworking brownie than he who dwelt at the Laird of Dalswinton's manor. The laird had a daughter, truly one of the fairest girls this side of the River Nith, and to whom the brownie of this story was fiercely attached.

Brownie nursed the lass as a small child and protected her from harm as she grew up to become an impressive-look-ing young woman. Her beauty was renowned throughout the countryside and she had many suitors. The laird's daughter used her many charms to flirt and play with the hearts of all the young lads that wooed her. Brownie, who was wise in the way of the world, advised her in matters of the heart and helped her in the beguiling of men. Thus, when the time came for her to marry, she had more than her share of hopeful lads from whom to choose a husband.

For all her feminine wiles, the laird's daughter was a virtuous maid and still innocent in the ways of the world on her wedding night.

So Brownie made himself invisible, and followed his lady into the bedchamber, where he whispered in her ear some things she should know, and even some things she shouldn't. So, instead of a dutiful maid filled with dread, the groom bedded a breathless bride who was as willing as she was wilful.

With Brownie's guidance the wedding night was a great success, so that when the time was just right, the fair maid-no-more awaited the birth of her first child. When the birthing pains were upon her, Brownie was ready. He ordered a simpleton servant to fetch a midwife, and then waited at his lady's side for the midwife to arrive. As his mistress's labors grew stronger and longer, so did her cries. Brownie could bear her anguished wailing no longer, nor the waiting either, so off he went to retrieve the much-needed midwife himself.

"It's so hard to find good help these days," he exclaimed in a fit. He wrapped himself in his lady's fur coat and, with fairy glamour for disguise, took the servant's horse from the stable. The half-witted hireling was still lacing his boot and was half asleep in the hay.

Brownie galloped apace to the midwife's place, which lay on the far side of the River Nith. The midwinter winds howled and the river raged, but he braved the foam and found his way to the midwife's croft at last. Brownie stole her from her meal of barley and bread, and carried her off on the horse. With the midwife in tow, he plunged into the river again, while the midwife screamed louder than his mistress who labored at home.

"Stay clear of the river pool, lest we meet a brownie there," warned the unsuspecting midwife to our crafty hero.

"No danger of that," replied he. "You've already met the only brownie you'll ever see."

They reached home safely. Brownie left the midwife to tend to his mistress as he went to the stable to unbridle the horse. Unbeknownst to him, a minister of the Church lay in hiding, waiting for his return. It seems the minister had convinced the laird that Brownie should be baptized and cleansed of his ungodly ways.

Poor Brownie. No sooner had he stabled the horse and begun his nightly chores, when out jumped the zealous minister, throwing holy water into Brownie's face, mumbling baptismal prayers all the while. Brownie yelped in horror. Never had he been so betrayed. He disappeared in a trice, like most brownies do, and was never seen again in that place.

The laird's fortunes were never as good again, for no mortal servant was as loyal or worked so willingly and hard as Brownie ever did. When Brownie vanished from the manor forever, so did all the fairy luck he possessed. As for the laird's lovely daughter, she became a fine wife and good mother and retained all that was left of Brownie's lucky legacy. She bore healthy children galore and was blithe for all the things that Brownie had taught her.

LEPRECHAUN
Abundance

THE IRISH LEPRECHAUN IS ONE of the most famous fairies in the world. He is a solitary, male fairy who stands about three feet high. His attire consists of a green waistcoat and breeches, woolen stockings, and buckled brogues. Sometimes he sports a large tricorn hat, a fashion borrowed from the invading English soldiers in the seventeenth century.

He is known as the fairy shoemaker because he is often spotted constructing shoes—but only ever one of a pair. He tends to be a surly fellow who fiercely guards his hoard of treasure, which usually consists of a large pot of gold, although he is also the owner of a magical pouch of coins that never empties, no matter how many coins are removed. If a mortal is able to capture a leprechaun, he or she may be able to coax the whereabouts of his treasure out of him, but the human must not take his eyes off him for an instant, lest the leprechaun disappear in an unguarded moment, along with all knowledge of his riches.

Money can certainly free a person of worry and material hardship, but it does not always make them happy. If the abundance a mortal longs for is purely monetary, the financial gains they make will provide only temporary happiness that is hard to maintain when the money is spent. People who invest in their inner lives and relationships, even if they are financially impoverished, are less likely to be adversely affected by the fluctuations of their bank account. If your actions and aspirations are honest and good, you will be eventually rewarded for your efforts, and the abundance you receive will have long-term effects.

The Leprechaun's Tale

ICHAEL WAS AN HONEST young man from a very poor family. He spent most of his time by himself, reading books or going for long walks along country roads. During his ambles through the countryside he dreamed of the day he could afford to live in a big, beautiful house with a fragrant garden full of flowers and a fabulous library full of books. But with so few prospects Michael did not know how this dream would come about. Despite his lowly circumstances, however, Michael was a cheerful lad, and never gave up hoping that he would find his fortune one day.

Michael was taking a pleasant stroll one summer day when he heard a faint tapping coming from the tall grasses that lined the side of the road. He approached the side of the road very carefully and gently parted the grass; here he spied a leprechaun hammering away on a single, small shoe. Michael had heard many tales about the hidden treasures of leprechauns, and how it was possible to capture one and force him to reveal the location of his hoard, so long as one did not look away for even so long as it took to bat an eye.

Michael quickly grabbed the little fellow and held tight as the leprechaun squirmed and struggled to get free.

"There's no use in strugglin', little man, 'cause I won't be lettin' ye free until ye tells me where ye've hidden your pot o' gold," cried Michael with glee.

"I'll not be able to tell ye much as long as ye're chokin' the life outa me," gasped the leprechaun, "so ye best leave me be."

The leprechaun sputtered and coughed so much that Michael was moved by the poor fellow's plight, so he let go of the little man and placed him gently on the ground, making sure not to lose sight of the leprechaun for a moment. Much to Michael's surprise, the leprechaun thanked him for his kindness. Leprechauns are normally well-known for their disagreeable natures. To keep himself occupied, and with his gaze fixed steadily upon the leprechaun, Michael related the story of his present misfortunes and his future hopes and dreams. When Michael had finished telling the leprechaun his personal history, the leprechaun looked warily upon the young boy for several moments before speaking.

"Ye're either tellin' the truth or ye're tellin' terrible lies. Since I'm thinkin' it's the truth ye told me, I'm willin' to prove to ye that not all leprechauns are the mean and miserly lot ye suppose us to be. Follow me and I'll show ye where I've hid me gold." No sooner had the leprechaun finished speaking than off he ran to the west, but not without Michael hard on his coat tails. The leprechaun ran hard and fast across many fields and meadows, Michael still in hot pursuit of him. Eventually they arrived at a fairy fort, where the leprechaun finally stopped running. Panting with exhaustion, the leprechaun pointed to one of the large boulders that lay on the hill.

"Ye'll find the crock o' gold if ye go through the crack in that rock there," said the leprechaun, "but ye best hurry up about it, 'cause there's not much time 'til the sun sets and then ye'll be trapped in the fort forever."

Duly warned, Michael followed the leprechaun through the narrow crack into the fort, where he spied a large pot of gold coins. He ran to the pot and dipped his hands in it, scooping up a fistful of its golden contents. "Rich, rich! I'll be rich for life!" Michael shouted.

"Some life if ye're stuck here for the rest of it!" the leprechaun retorted. "There's only a few minutes before the sun sets and the crack in the rock closes. Collect what ye need now before there's no way out." Michael tried to lift the pot of gold but it was too heavy and did not budge. So he quickly gathered as many gold coins as his pockets could hold and managed to escape through the crack only seconds before the last rays of the sun disappeared below the horizon and the entrance to the fort slammed shut. When Michael looked back at the fort, the leprechaun was nowhere to be seen.

Michael lived in peace and prosperity for the rest of his life. He never saw the leprechaun again but was reminded of the little fellow every time he reached into his coat pockets for money, for there was no end to the supply of gold coins that he had found in the fairy fort.

LUTIN

Whimsy

THE MOST COMMON FAIRIES of northern France are lutins. They are small sprites and appear to be related to the English hobgoblin or lob, but usually deny any relationship with their cousins across the channel, despite all evidence to the contrary. One thing is for certain though, they are utterly unpredictable and quite whimsical.

Lutins demonstrate distinctly male characteristics, especially their fondness for attractive mortal females and playing practical jokes. One of their most common pranks is the inextricable snarling and tangling of horses' manes or girls' tresses (although lutins prefer to think of it as braiding).

Lutins are superb shapeshifters. They most frequently transform themselves into horses, fully bridled and saddled, luring people to ride them, and then quickly casting them off into the nearest ditch or stream. They have also been known to take on the appearance of spiders or goats. Most confounding of all is that lutins can be very helpful to needy mortals and then abruptly change tactics in midcourse, wreaking havoc among the very people they started to assist.

Lutins are by no means the only fairies known for their fickle behavior; fickleness is probably the most consistent and widespread of all fairy traits. A whimsical person is impetuous and imaginative, which are definite fairy-friendly traits. Children can be whimsical with impunity. The same behavior in adults is often childish and irresponsible, and almost always unreliable. It is a rare and special person who is both dependable and capricious. Such mortals receive blessings from both this world and the other.

The Lutin's Tale

MARIE-CLAIRE WAS AN only child and spent much of her time alone. She learned at a very young age how to keep herself busy and entertained. One of her greatest pleasures was grooming the family horse, Coco. Marie-Claire spent many happy hours in the barn with Coco, brushing his coat until it shone and whispering all sorts of sweet, little endearments into his long ears that were as soft as satin.

As Marie-Claire grew older and began to blossom into a lovely young maid, her fondness for grooming Coco began to sour. She still loved Coco, of course, and still enjoyed stroking his broad flanks and blowing into his large ears, but his mane had developed tangles that were impossible to undo. Sometimes his mane was so gnarled with knots and lumps that the only thing she could do was cut it.

This continued for months until Marie-Claire discovered the reason for Coco's unruly mane. One morning she arrived earlier than usual for Coco's morning ration of oats and what did she see but a funny-looking little man sitting on the horse's neck, making a complete mess of his mane. As soon as the strange little

fellow caught sight of Marie-Claire, he jumped down from the horse and scampered out of the barn in the blink of an eye.

At last Marie-Claire knew the reason for Coco's tangled mane. Several years passed and still the silly sprite pestered Coco and Marie-Claire with his pranks. Sometimes he would change himself into a frisky mare and tease poor Coco mercilessly. It seemed he never tired of the same old tricks, night after night. But Marie-Claire did. She had less and less time for the troublesome little man because mortal men began to occupy her thoughts instead. She had grown up to be one of the most sought-after girls in the town where she lived. She was charming, pretty, and bright, and no longer alone. Coco missed the attention of his beloved mistress and, unbeknownst to Marie-Claire, the little lutin missed her even more.

The day came when Marie-Claire married the best of all her suitors, a fine young man named Gilles. Gilles knew how to make her happy, which was to give her time to be alone. Most men would have found Marie-Claire's independence a fault but it only made Gilles more fond of her. Marie-Claire was happiest when she could drift off into a world of her own, just as she had done as a young girl. Every night she spent long hours at her spinning wheel in front of the hearth, humming softly to herself and dreaming of days to come.

One evening, as she sat in the warm glow of the fire, she heard another voice join in her humming. When she looked up from her spinning, whom should she see sitting on a stool next to her but the funny little man who had badgered poor Coco for so long. He gazed into her eyes more fondly than she had ever seen Gilles do.

"I have missed you so much, *ma belle*," said he. "Who is the man who has taken you away from me?"

"Myself did that," said Marie-Claire slyly. "No one but myself would ever do such a thing."

The lutin (for that is what he was) stayed until Marie-Claire shooed him away with an iron poker. But he returned again the next night, and the night after that, until finally Marie-Claire told Gilles about the little pest.

Gilles did not mind Marie-Claire keeping to herself but he would not let her spend good time with anyone else, and that was that. The very next evening Gilles prepared to receive their unwelcome guest. He heated an iron plate until it was unbearably hot and placed it on the stool where the little man sat. Then, dressed in Marie-Claire's clothes, he took his place at the spinning wheel and made a pretence of spinning. The lutin, however, was not the stupid fool that Gilles had taken him for, and saw through the man's pathetic ruse immediately.

"Where is *ma belle*?" asked the little man, as he took his usual seat. Before Gilles could answer him, the lutin jumped off the stool, screaming in pain.

"Ouch! My bottom is badly burned!" he bellowed. He ran swiftly across the room and out the door, joining a band of his friends who waited for him outside. He pranced back and forth, nursing his burning bottom wailing oh so woefully.

"Who burned you?" his fairy friends asked him, with more curiosity than concern.

"Myself, it was myself!" he squealed. Silly lutin. He never lived that comment down. And he never troubled Marie-Claire again.

PERI

Madness

ERIS ARE THE ENTICINGLY lovely female spirits of ancient Persia. Like numerous fairies the world over, peris have a dual nature —sometimes they are benevolent and at other times they create mischief and mayhem. With the arrival of Islam, peris were demoted to the rank of fallen angels, though they continued to perform kind deeds for needy mortals. Their usual form is typically diminutive and humanlike; they are excellent shapeshifters as well. They are ethereal creatures who feed on exotic perfumes, which also serve to repel their enemies, the malevolent deevs.

There are numerous stories of peris being taken as wives by mortal men, a trait shared by the Scottish selkie and the Welsh Gwragedd Annwn. The accompanying story is remarkable for its similarity to the selkie tale, especially regarding the concealment of the peri wife's fairy garment by her mortal husband.

When mortals encounter fairies, they have entered a space that is either part of the Otherworld or one that lies at its threshold. Upon returning to ordinary time and space, mortals are almost always psychologically altered. Madness is sometimes one of the more unfortunate results of such an encounter. In the case of human–fairy marriages, it is usually an obsessive, all-consuming love on the part of the mortal that eventually leads to uncontrollable grief and torment. Persian folklore refers to this condition as "peri-stricken."

Love is a form of possession. Couples in love often describe themselves as mad about each other, but love for an Otherworld spirit is even more maddening.

The Peri's Tale

A YOUNG MERCHANT, SEEKING fame and fortune, took a brief respite from his travels one day. He settled beneath a tree by the banks of a gently flowing stream and spent a quiet afternoon pondering his future. The sun was casting a pale-pink glow across the horizon when four milk-white doves descended from the branches of the tree under which he sat, landing not far from where he rested.

Much to his amazement, the four birds transformed themselves into graceful, delicate young women. They removed their gossamer garments and entered the water to bathe. As they laughed and played in the shallow stream, the young man stole their clothes and hid them in the hollow of the tree. Then he waited and watched for the fair maidens to finish their ablutions, which was no hardship at all.

When the maidens discovered that their clothes were missing they began to lament, for they could not leave without their magical finery. The peris (for that is what they were) looked high and low for their robes, until at last they noticed the merchant hiding behind a tree. They knew at once he was responsible for taking their outfits and beseeched him to return them. But the merchant was a lonely man and declared that he would not do so unless one of the fair maids promised to marry him.

The sisters explained that such a union was not possible, for they were made from ether and he was made of clay. But the young man could not listen to reason because he was under the spell of uncontrollable desire. After much fruitless pleading, the desperate maids agreed to his terms.

The merchant selected the youngest and most beautiful to be his bride. The hapless peri wailed profusely but to no avail, for the young man would not be moved. The peri's sisters consoled her as best they could. Finally, they donned their magic robes and flew away, leaving their sister to grieve alone.

Delighted with his new bride, the merchant brought her to his home and dressed her in beautiful raiments of silk and satin. He took great care, however, to hide her fairy robe where she would never find it. He did his best to win her affections but for a long time she was desolate. Eventually, however, the patience and kindness of her husband won her over. Or so it seemed. When at last she bore him a child, and then another, the merchant was finally certain of her love and devotion.

When he believed that he had finally secured the peri's love, the merchant was delirious with joy. Once a very serious young man, the merchant became a fool in love, child-like and irresponsible. His friends observed the change in him, and shook their heads and clicked their tongues with mock pity.

Ten years of marital bliss passed until one day the merchant found himself financially embar-rassed, no doubt because he had been so distracted with love for his lovely fairy wife. Circumstances made it neces-sary for him to travel abroad once more. Before departing on his voyage, the merchant employed the services of a chaperone to look after his wife. The elderly guardian came with an excellent reputation, so the merchant entrusted her with information on the true nature of his peri wife and the place where he had hidden her fairy dress with its magical powers.

Her husband's departure distressed the peri wife, for she became wistful and anxious. At least that was how the elderly chaperone perceived the situation. The elderly woman consoled her charge with reminders that the husband's absence was only temporary. This only seemed to distress the peri more. Matters continued in this vein until one day, seeing the peri as she bathed in perfumed waters, the old woman expressed her admiration for the girl aloud, apparently forgetting that her ward was no ordinary mortal.

"My good woman," said the peri to her chaperone, "if you would like to see me in my true glory, as the Maker had intended, you must bring me my native garment forthwith."

The simple woman retrieved the magic garment from its hiding place and presented it to the peri. The peri donned the dress straightaway and, like a captive bird released from its cage, she spread her wings and flew out of her bedroom window into the freedom of the open skies. She was never seen again.

When the merchant returned from his jour-ney and learned that his wife had left him, he fell into deep despair. The light of his life had gone. From that day forward, he remained shut away in his house, unable to cope with the mundane affairs of living. With the loss of his only love he had lost his wits as well.

LEANAN SIDHE

Inspiration

THE LEANAN SIDHE (PRONOUNCED LANAWN SHEE) is a solitary, seductive Irish spirit whose name means "fairy mistress." She is also known in a more malevolent version as Lhiannanshee on the Isle of Man. The Leanan Sidhe is a source of inspiration and vision to favored mortals. Always ethereal and enigmatic, she will alter her appearance to become the epitome of beauty for any artist-lover she chooses.

She is the fairy muse of poets and musicians and rewards mortals who fall under her spell with fame and fortune. Artists influenced by the Leanan Sidhe create their most inspired works, but usually pay dearly for it. Where the Manx variant sucks the blood from her victims, the Leanan Sidhe gradually extracts the life force from the mortals she serves. Her mortal disciples frequently burn themselves out, eventually expiring from exhaustion or going mad from brain fever.

Karmic laws exact a heavy toll for mortals who acquire goods from across the border of the Otherworld, especially if it is for inspiration. The root of the word "inspire" comes from the Latin *spiritus*, meaning breath, life, or spirit. Being inspired by Leanan Sidhe intensifies mortal life force. Life becomes immediate and deeply felt. Fairy morality is not as yielding as ours, so if humans expire because they have drawn from the Otherworld for inspiration, it is a fair exchange.

Leanan Sidhe teaches mortals to seek inspiration in the seemingly ordinary, everyday world, which is more interesting and diverse than most mortals ever realize. Truly inspired people are able to create magic out of the mundane.

The Leanan Sidhe's Tale

FREDERICK CLAIBORNE WAS weary of the fawning, simpering men and women of the social elite who gathered around him at artistic salons and soirées. His attendance at these affairs always attracted a great deal of fuss, as he was increasingly intoxicated and rude, even to his most ardent admirers. His appearances always inflamed the rumors that he was a brilliant young composer who was frittering his talents away on licentious, self-destructive behavior.

Frederick's last opera, *The Devil's Advocate*, had been received with great enthusiasm and esteem, but that was almost two years ago. His fading popularity was based on his former achievements, dashing good looks, and debonair charm. When he was not disrupting the civility of the better salons of society patrons, he was out carousing in brothels and opium dens by himself.

He found himself at Mrs. Axworthy's Annual Society Benefit and Ball for the Arts—yet another tedious affair—when he met the Lady Leanna. He had hidden in the library to drink his Scotch in peace when Lady Leanna suddenly appeared out of nowhere.

"I'm so sorry, I hope I'm not disturbing you," said Lady Leanna. Before Frederick could apply his caustic wit to deter the intruder, Lady Leanna smiled. She was a woman of subtle beauty and daring style. Her thick mane of chestnut brown hair hung loosely down around her shoulders, a most becoming, if somewhat inappropriate fashion for a woman of her enticingly indeterminate years.

Lady Leanna was the wife of the aged and ailing Lord Samuel Shelby, or so she said. Though obviously a woman of wealth and position, Frederick wanted nothing more than to spend time with her in sparkling, convivial conversation. By the end of the evening, Lady Leanna had agreed to finance Frederick while he wrote his new opera. She was very familiar with his work and seemed more interested in him as an artist than an amour, which was a welcome change for Frederick.

Their conversation was briefly interrupted when a lusty young couple burst into the library. The couple left swiftly, sniggering at Frederick for having so thoroughly destroyed his mind with excessive indulgence that he had taken to conversing with invisible companions.

The next day, Frederick was looking for a curative that would ease the thrashing in his skull when he heard an assured, gentle knock at his door. It was the Lady Leanna. She wanted to see where he worked and talk to him about his new opera. They spent most of the afternoon at his grand piano, playing and singing some of the great arias of the day, including a few of his own. Lady Leanna was a coloratura soprano who demonstrated an extraordinary facility for bel canto. Frederick did not understand why she had not pursued a career in opera. Lady Leanna replied that she had more important work to do, though what it was, she declined to say.

Lady Leanna called on Frederick several afternoons a week. He always had something to show her as he feverishly worked through what he knew would be his finest work ever. Frederick was composing as he had never done before, not only from a renewed sense of commitment, but also because he no longer worked in a haze of whiskey fumes. He had never felt so clearheaded or singleminded of purpose.

Between Lady Leanna's visits, Frederick wrote incessantly, barely stopping to eat or sleep. Formerly a *bon vivant*, he was now a

recluse. Four months after meeting Lady Leanna, Frederick's opera was finished and, to look at him, it seemed he was too. Although his soul soared, he had also physically deteriorated.

Frederick was ecstatic when he finally presented the complete score and libretto to Lady Leanna. They spent the afternoon at the piano, playing and singing the opera from beginning to end. As the final strains of the dying hero's aria still lingered between them, Lady Leanna, whose behavior was always beyond reproach, leaned close to Frederick and whispered in his ear, "You have moved me deeply, my dear Mr. Claiborne. May I thank you with a kiss?" Her invitation, like everything else about her, was irresistible. He succumbed willingly. The last thing that Frederick Claiborne felt was Lady Leanna's mouth on his.

Frederick Claiborne's posthumous opera, *Child of the Muse*, premiered at the Royal Opera House. It was agreed that it was a work of genius and one that secured his place in the pantheon of great operatic composers. But there was much speculation and myth about the dedication: "For Lady Leanna Shelby, My Love and Light." No one knew who she was, or if she even existed.

SELKIE

Longing

SELKIES ARE THE SEAL FAIRIES native to the Orkney and Shetland Islands north of Scotland. In Ireland and the Hebrides they are referred to as roane. They retain their seal shapes so that they can swim to their underwater caves in the sea. Occasionally they will come ashore, shed their seal-skins, and dance together in the moonlight as beautiful maidens. Seal maidens can be identified in human form by their soft, dark seal-like eyes.

Like the Welsh Gwragedd Annwn, selkies will sometimes marry mortals. If a man is able steal the skin of a selkie, she will mate with him. Children born of such a union have webbed hands and feet. Should the selkie spouse find her sealskin again, she will assume her seal form at once and return to her home in the sea.

While the selkie is captive in her human form, she constantly longs to return to the sea, no matter how dutiful a wife and mother she may be. She is never completely at home with her life on land, for the call of the sea is much stronger than any attachments she may have to her mortal family.

The longing a selkie feels for her rightful home is akin to the feeling mortals have when they are homesick (even if it is for a place not yet known to them) or separated from their loved ones. The lesson of the selkie is that constant yearning is a sure sign of where the heart belongs. Maintaining appearances for the sake of acceptance doesn't lead to fulfilling one's birthright. Pay heed to the call of your heart.

The Selkie's Tale

ON THE EDGE OF THIS WORLD lies a lonely island with a memory as long as the sea is deep. On this island there once lived a solitary fisherman who longed for the company of a wife and children, so that his stories would not die with him. He would walk for many hours along the rocky shores of the island, pondering his lonely fate. One night, on a full moon in May, he spied thirteen slender, graceful maidens dancing by the edge of the sea. They were dressed only in the shimmering light of the moon. Not far from where the maidens danced the fisherman found thirteen silky soft sealskins. He took one of the skins and kept it at his side while he watched the maidens dance to the rhythmic beating of the waves that washed ashore.

When the maidens ceased their dancing, each one donned one of the pelts they had cast aside for their revelries. One of the fair ones was unable to find her skin and began to lament as the other seal maidens returned to the waves without her. At last she noticed the fisherman who held her skin in his hands. She begged him to return the skin to her but he would not. He had found in her a wife who would make him a proper home. Without her skin there was naught that the seal maiden could do but follow the fisherman.

She became the fisherman's faithful wife and bore him four children, all of whom had webs between their fingers and toes. The fairy mother tended her children with great devotion and took them to swim in the sea each day where her sisters kept constant vigil. The children made friends with the seals that would watch them as they played in the foam.

For many years the fairy wife lived this way. She never complained or suffered aloud but there was always a sadness in her dark, distant eyes. At night, and especially when the full moon shone, she would often steal away to the place where she had last danced with her sisters from the sea. And there she would stand, long through the night, gazing out upon the dark waters. She shed no tears, nor did she smile, but sometimes she would sing a plaintive song, so that her sisters would draw near to the shore, and join in her lament.

Her days were filled with the business of her everyday life. One day, as she washed and cleaned the home she had tended with such diligence for so many years, her children tumbled out of the loft where they had been playing. They clamored enthusiastically around their fairy mother, "See, Mama, see what we have found. It is a sealskin as fine and soft as a newborn pup's." The eldest child, a boy of fifteen, held a seal pelt in his hands.

Their fairy mother stared at the fine folds of fur draped over her son's arm. She recognized at once the skin her mortal husband had seized from her so long ago. She took the coat gratefully, telling her children how she would put it to good use straightaway. There was no point in keeping such a fine pelt hidden away in the loft, she told them. She left them with instructions to look after the cottage while she went to cleanse the dust of the years from the pelt. As she looked into the eyes of her children one last time she saw the past and future meet. They waved and shouted happily after their mother, pleased with the special gift that had so gladdened her heart.

Their mother did not look back. Her eyes remained fixed ahead of her as she hastened to the rocky beach where her mortal life had begun barely a generation ago. She stood upon the shore and sighed to see the familiar, sunlit waters; they had not sparkled so brightly for a very long time. In the distance, peering over the spray, a dozen pairs of soulful black eyes waited and watched for her.

Although the selkie grieved to leave her children, the call of the sea was more than she could bear. Over time, she knew she would visit her children and make certain that they would never hunger for want of fish.

"I have come home," she whispered to the waves. Then she let her mortal garments slide upon the rocky ground, donned her shiny fur coat and slipped silently into the sea.

GWRAGEDD ANNWN

Devotion

THE GWRAGEDD ANNWN (pronounced grageth anoon) are beautiful water spirits who dwell in the deep lakes of the Black Mountains in Wales. They are predominantly female and can be identified by their tall, slender bodies and long, blonde hair. Unlike most water spirits, who share both the life-sustaining and life-taking properties of their natural element, the Gwragedd Annwn are completely benign.

Their grace and beauty are irresistible to men, who have been known to take them as wives. The Gwragedd prove to be loyal spouses and devoted mothers but the marriages usually end because of the stupidity of the husbands. The union is dissolved immediately if the husband strikes the wife three times. Complying with this taboo can be very difficult for the husband, considering the strange, fairy ways of his wife, which can often be frustrating.

The Gwragedd clearly demonstrate the lesson of devotion. Unfortunately, most mortals are not capable of unconditional love or devotion, although it is the kind of love most people long for. Humans need only look to their animal companions, such as a beloved dog or cat, to behold the complete trust and unconditional love we want from each other. In its loftiest form it is the sort of love we seek when we commune with the divine, but so few attain it. Saints, mystics, and people of profound and unswerving faith are the fortunate few who experience such rapture, and not without considerable sacrifice.

In order to receive such love, we must first give it, and give it freely.

The Gwragedd Annwn's Tale

ON A WARM SPRING EVENING a very long time ago, a young Welsh farmer rested on the shore of a mountain lake while his cattle grazed nearby. The lake was one of many that can be found in the Black Mountains. As the last rays of the setting sun sparkled on the deep waters, the young man spied a lovely maiden sitting upon a rock as she combed her long, golden hair. All at once and without warning the young man was smitten with love for the fair maid. He offered her some bread, entreating her to come ashore and join him. She took one look at the bread and declared that it was too hard, whereupon she dived into the lake.

That night at home the young man told the tale of his encounter with the fairy maiden to his widowed mother. There was a wistful longing in his voice as he spoke. Feeling compassion for her son, his mother gave him some unbaked dough and instructed him to return to the lake and try his luck with the fair maid again. The next day he did as his mother bade him but the maiden found the dough too soft. So, the following day, the young man returned for a third time with a loaf of his mother's lightly baked bread. When he showed the soft bread to his ladylove, she looked pleased, but disappeared beneath the waves without a word. Before the young man had time fully to comprehend his loss, a noble-looking, elderly man appeared on the surface of the lake. With him were his two daughters, identical in appearance and bearing to the maid with whom the young man had become so enamored.

The Lord of the Lake told the young man that he would grant him permission to marry his daughter if he could identify his chosen love. The poor farmer was about to give up in despair when one of the maids moved her foot very slightly, revealing beneath the folds of her dress the peculiar lacing of her sandals, which he recognized immediately.

The fairy maiden was duly promised to the mortal on the condition that he would lose both his wife and her dowry if he struck her three times, no matter for what reason. The dowry consisted of as many animals as the fairy maiden could count in a single breath. Although she was unable to count past five, the young couple received a respectable dowry of five fat, healthy cows, five horses, five pigs, and five sheep. The couple married and were happy, and the fairy wife bore her husband three fine sons. But sometimes her perverse fairy nature prevailed. She would weep on joyous occasions and laugh when others mourned, as at a child's funeral, which would cause her husband to reprimand her with a gentle tap. When he eventually rebuked her in this way a third time, she turned to him and said, "You have struck me for the last time. Never will you see me again!" She left for her palace home at the bottom of the lake with all the farm animals in tow, including a slaughtered calf that magically came back to life.

Her husband pined for her until the day he died. His sons, however, were not abandoned by their fairy mother. She visited them frequently and taught them the secrets of herbal medicine, which they passed on to their children, who, in turn, passed them on to theirs. The fairy descendants eventually became well-known for their healing abilities, and their services were much sought after. The physicians of Mydfai were considered to be the finest physicians in the land and the legacy of their healing powers continued for many generations.

RUSALKI

Seduction

MANY OF THE MOST TREACHEROUS fairies are spirits whose primary habitat is water. The Russian rusalki are amphibious female fairies whose principle residences during the dark months of winter are found in freshwater lakes or rivers. During the summer they come ashore to dance and dwell in the leafy woods.

They are lovely pale creatures with luxurious, long, green hair. They do not like to wear clothing but when they do, their garments of choice are the sheerest of white dresses that may be adorned with leaves or reeds. Their most prized possession is a magic comb that gives them the ability to conjure magic and cast spells. The comb is an important magical tool for water nymphs far and wide, including the Welsh Gwragedd Annwn.

A mortal man who mates with a rusalki will experience a bliss he has never known with a mortal lover. Unfortunately, things invariably end badly for the man. Lured into the rusalki's watery abode, the mortal man enters into a physical embrace with his fairy lover. These moments of physical rapture are usually his last. The man dies in the arms of the rusalki, whose final, dubious act of love draws the last breath of life from him.

Seduction is an extremely pleasurable experience and has little to do with logic or reason, because very basic, immediate forces are at work when a person manipulates or succumbs to love, money, or power. It doesn't matter if the person is the temptor or the tempted, both parties engage in a selfish act motivated almost exclusively by overpowering desire.

The Rusalki's Tale

THERE ONCE LIVED A handsome Russian prince who, despite his position and wealth, was a lonely man. His family and friends did not understand his sadness, for he had more possessions than most people could ever dream of owning. To prevent his melancholy from infecting others, the prince kept himself to himself, leaving affairs of state in the capable hands of his noblemen and court advisors.

He enjoyed hunting and would spend many hours pursuing deer and boar in the great forests of his northern kingdom. One morning in early summer, while hunting wild swan, he spied a beautiful woman dancing in a forest clearing. She was so graceful and light on her feet that they barely touched the ground. Her long, unbound hair was the color of leaves in the early spring, and whirled all about her with a life of its own, as if participating in her ecstatic dance. The prince watched the gorgeous creature, who was a rusalki, dance until she fell exhausted upon the ground. The prince ran to her aid but stopped short when he saw her produce a comb out of thin air and begin to smooth her hair. The comb, carved from the

bone or tusk of an animal, seemed to sing a thin, haunting melody as she pulled it through her tresses. With each stroke of the comb the prince became more entranced with the form of the rusalki, so that when she finished her task and spread her lavish locks of hair across her pale shoulders and back, he was barely able to recall his own name or who he was.

The rusalki seemed unaware of the prince's presence until she suddenly turned and faced him in all her splendor. Her eyes, which were greener than the darkest emeralds, filled with tears. The prince, who was a kind man, quickly pulled himself out of his reverie and asked the nymph what troubled her.

"I am grieved by your melancholy," she replied very softly. "I can help to ease your pain, if you would let me…" The prince was amazed that the rusalki seemed to know exactly what was in his heart.

"How can you help me?" he asked.

"Come, lie down here with me," the rusalki replied, as she lay down in soft, dew-covered moss beneath the boughs of a great oak. Without a moment's hesitation, the prince did as he was told. As he lay with his ladylove beneath the tree, the prince vowed to himself that this was the woman he would marry. He pulled his lover closer in their embrace and proposed to her. Her eyes misted over again and she replied sadly that she would not marry a man who could not be faithful. The prince was deeply wounded by her remark and wept profusely, assuring her that such a thing would never happen. The rusalki was unmoved by his tears. But the prince begged and pleaded. Never had he wanted anything so much as the ravishing creature who lay in his arms. Finally, after many tears and promises from the prince, the rusalki relented and eventually agreed to marry the prince.

The prince and his fairy bride lived together in wedded bliss for almost a year. The courtiers were happy for their prince, who had become more active in the affairs of state. But one of the ladies-in-waiting was jealous of the prince's newfound happiness, for she had been in love with him for many years. So one night the jealous woman gave the prince a magic potion, which caused him to break his marriage vows and his pact with his fairy wife.

The very next day the rusalki was gone. The guilt-ridden, grief-stricken prince set out immediately to look for his wife. He looked high and low in the forests and mountains where he had first seen her, but to no avail. A full month had passed until he found her at last, sitting by the shore of a lake, combing her hair. The prince fell to his knees and begged her forgiveness. She was mercilessly silent and unmoved as he prostrated himself before her. At length she left him and swam into the lake.

"I will ease your suffering. Follow me," she said, before she dived beneath the waves. The prince followed her to the bottom of the lake where she lived. In her watery home made from long, slender reeds the two lovers embraced. The prince heaved a sigh of relief and gratitude as his wife's arms went round him.

The rusalki wrapped herself around him tightly. Her arms held his head to hers, her legs entwined with his. Wrapped in his lover's embrace, the prince could not tell where his body ended and the body of his fairy wife began.

"I could die in such rapture," the prince whispered softly to his rusalki love.

"So be it," said the rusalki. Then she pulled him still closer to her bosom, where he spent his final, ecstatic breath.

MALA VILA

Betrayal

T HE SPIRITS OF THE WOODS, lakes, and streams of the Balkan States are known as vilas. They are lithe and lovely maidens with long, flowing hair who act as guardians of their forest domain. Like most wood and water nymphs, they love to dance in sylvan glades by the light of the moon. Vilas are usually benign but will punish mortals with deadly arrows if the privacy of their revels is invaded. They are also excellent herbalists and healers. Their companion animals are deer, on which they have been seen riding through the woods.

The mala vila (*mala* means "little" in Serbian) of the following story is much smaller than her sister spirits of the woods and more passive in her behavior toward mortal men. Despite her fragile appearance and demeanor, mortals still suffer the consequences of mistreating her. The lesson in the mala vila's tale is one of the most difficult lessons a mortal can learn. A betrayal of trust is a deeply emotional, heart-wrenching experience. It sullies the reputation of supposedly trustworthy people, sometimes forever. Often something as simple as a broken promise can feel like a betrayal.

Words have enormous power. When spoken aloud they express human feelings and thoughts. If words are spoken in the form of a promise or oath, the word becomes a bond between two or more people. Breaking a promise, like breaking a spell, severs ties that are often impossible to mend.

The Mala Vila's Tale

LONG AGO AND FAR AWAY there lived a great king and queen who had only one son. The handsome prince was the pride and joy of his parents and the sole heir to the throne. When he came of age the king spared no expense for the celebrations. Hundreds of important people from all over the land came to the palace to honor the prince on his birthday.

Everyone celebrated with much feasting, singing, and dancing in the splendid halls of the royal palace. The happy night quickly drew to an end, and when the last exhausted reveler had gone, the prince took a solitary walk in the quiet of the palace garden.

The prince heard the last stroke of midnight toll when he spied a pale light emanating from a grove of birch trees. Upon closer inspection the prince saw a tiny, delicate woman, no bigger than a doll, standing beneath the silver trees under the glow of the full moon. At once the prince recognized the extraordinary creature to be a very small vila, or fairy.

The tiny fairy told the prince that she had been invited to the ball but did not come for fear of being trampled beneath the revelers' feet.

"So I have come to honor you here in the moonlit garden where I am safe and happy," she explained, and then she curtsied. As the prince bent closer to speak with her, she disappeared in a trice.

Enchanted by the fairy maiden, the prince returned to the garden the following night to look for her. Sure enough, the fairy was waiting for him. They spent the evening together, engrossed in each other's company and deep in conversation. As they walked and talked, the prince noticed that the fairy maiden gradually grew in size as the evening progressed. By the time they parted, the fairy was twice the size she had been when the prince first met her.

The two sweethearts continued to meet in the garden every night after that. And each night the fairy maiden continued to grow in stature, until at last she was the size of a normal human being. As the fairy grew, so did the love the prince felt for her. It wasn't long before he asked her to be his bride. The fairy replied that she would marry him under the condition that he promise to remain true only to her. It was no hardship for the prince to promise her what she asked, for he was besotted with her.

"Remember," said the fairy, "I shall always stay true to you just as long as you promise to stay true to your word."

The prince was overjoyed at his good fortune. He introduced his future wife to his parents the very next day, who were happy that their only son had found true love with such a sweet and proper young woman. The happy couple married within a week with great pomp and ceremony. For seven years they lived together in wedded bliss. Then the king suddenly took ill and died.

The funeral was attended by hundreds of mourners, many of whom were elegant lady courtiers. The most elegant woman of all had a thick mane of curly red hair, skin the color of alabaster, and eyes as black as coal. She was a witch who had come to the funeral seeking to seduce the prince. The witch was admired by everyone there but especially the prince, for whose sake she had magically devised her charms.

As the funeral procession made its way to the graveyard, the prince cast his eyes upon the enticing enchantress twice. When he looked her way a third time, his fairy wife, who had been walking at his side, tripped over her dress.

"This dress is too long for me," she apologized. The prince barely took notice, for by then he was completely enamored by the red-haired beauty. The princess grew smaller and smaller as the cortège continued on its path. By the time the procession passed the birch grove where the prince and his fairy wife had met, the mala vila, who by that time was no bigger than a doll, simply vanished.

But the prince paid no heed. He was under the spell of the witch. Within a week they married, for he had completely forgotten about his fairy love, so powerful was the spell cast by his new wife. Within three days, however, the spell was broken and so was the prince's heart. The witch proved very quickly that she had only desired the wealth and power that came with her royal husband. Barely a month had passed before the prince could stand his new wife's coldness and greed no longer, whereupon he banished her out of his sight and from court forever.

Left alone, the prince grieved deeply for the fairy wife he had betrayed. Every night he went to the birch grove and called her name, but she never returned. He pined for his lost love until the day he died, a very old and lonely man.

THE WORLD OF FAIRIES

ELLE MAID
Addiction

ELLE FOLK ARE SCANDINAVIAN FAIRIES whose preferred habitat is the windswept moors of their native country, eponymously named elle-moors. The males are bearded old men, sporting close-fitting hats, and are usually shorter than the females. The females stand less than five feet high and have long, blonde hair; this hides their most distinguishing feature, a hollow back.

Elle maids enjoy singing to the accompaniment of a lyre, which they play superbly. Mortal men who hear the soulful strains of the elle maid's music are very quickly caught in her spell. Humans are not the only mortals who should be wary of elle folk. If a cow grazes where the elle folk have left bodily fluids, such as spit (or worse), it will sicken and die. The only cure for cattle that have eaten tainted grass is a dose of St. John's Wort, harvested at midnight.

A mortal who partakes of fairy food or drink will remain trapped in the fairy realm indefinitely. Once there, mortals lose all sense of time and experience a euphoria that is highly addictive, and a large part of the reason they long to go back for more when they return to this reality. A mortal does not need to have been caught in the Otherworld, however, to know that escapist preoccupations can lead to overindulgence and excess. The desire to leave behind the daily grind of existence and find solace in dreamy pleasure is universal, but it is a temporary solution that frequently takes a heavy toll on a person's health and well-being.

The Elle Maid's Tale

A FARMER'S SON WAS TENDING a herd of cows in a pasture that bordered on land where elle folk were reputed to live. So when the young man, whose name was Torvald, saw a fair, young maid approach him as he watched over his herd, he knew to be on his guard, for she was probably an elle maid. She came to him all smiles and grace but he steeled himself against her charms and witchy ways.

"You look as if you might be thirsty," said the maid. "I have fresh milk, if you would like it," she offered.

Torvald tried very hard to ignore the fairy maiden but that was difficult to do because she was so pretty. Then Torvald reasoned that she might not be an elle maid at all, and to know for certain he need only look at her back and see if it were hollow. The elle maid danced and sang for him most alluringly as he pondered these things. She was truly a pleasure to behold but he noticed how she was careful not to turn her back to him. Torvald concluded that she must surely be an elle maid, so he strengthened his resolve to refuse any food or drink with which she might tempt him.

When the elle maid perceived that Torvald could not be moved by her singing and dancing, she stopped, placed her hands on her hips, and sighed in resignation. Her sigh was like the tinkling of chimes carried on a summer wind. The more obvious it became to Torvald that she was indeed a fairy, the more determined he became not to succumb to her charms. The elle maid tilted her head and smiled sweetly at him. All of a sudden she pulled up her shirt to reveal a pair of pert, round breasts with nipples as pink as rosebuds in May.

"You may suckle my breasts for milk, if you'd like," she cajoled.

Well, that was that. Torvald was unable to resist any longer. He leapt upon the maid with a hunger he had not known since he was an infant crying at his mother's breast. The milk was warm and sweet to the taste. But sweeter yet was the blissful serenity that washed over him as he lay at the bosom of the elle maid. When he had his fill, the fairy took him by the hand and led him across the moors. He followed the elle maid willingly.

For three days and nights Torvald lived with the elle maid in her home beneath a grassy

THE ELLE MAID'S TALE

hill. He was indulged in every earthly pleasure imaginable. Torvald had never known how eating, drinking, bathing, and even sleeping could be such sensuous delights. He indulged the maid in all her strange whims, as she did him. The young man lost all sense of time but he no longer cared: Torvald had found heaven on earth.

Meanwhile, Torvald's mother and father were frantic with worry. They had correctly surmised that their son had been a victim of fairy enchantment and feared that he would never return. On the morning of the fourth day of Torvald's disappearance, his father was tending cattle in the same place where his son had met his fairy lover. As the farmer gazed out over the landscape, he discerned a man far off in the distance, making his way to the farm. Moments later the farmer recognized his son. Torvald, it seemed, had been turned away by the elle maid who had grown weary of his company and had moved onto better things.

With a yelp of joy the farmer ran back to the house and ordered his wife to cook some beef. Torvald's mother threw a large portion of meat on the fire and then anxiously awaited the arrival of her son. Torvald arrived at the farmhouse a short while later. Without a word of explanation he sat down at the kitchen table as if nothing had happened. Torvald's mother also said nothing as she placed the roasted meat before him. Torvald sniffed at the food disdainfully and said he knew a place where he could find much tastier treats. Suddenly Torvald's father gave his son a blow on the side of the head, shouting "Eat! Eat!" until at last the poor, beleaguered lad was obliged to do so.

Upon finishing the last morsel of meat, Torvald fell into a deep sleep. He awoke from his slumber three days later, much to his parent's relief. But the joy they felt for the return of their son was short-lived. Torvald did not know who he was, or where he was, for he had gone quite mad.

SUCCUBUS

Nightmare

THE SUCCUBUS IS A TERRIFYING female spirit who visits mortal men while they sleep, inducing nightmares of a highly sexual nature. During the Middle Ages she represented all that Christianity considered to be sinful and evil. The succubus was one of the most demonized spirits of the medieval world because she was a temptress symbolizing humanity's fall from grace.

Succubi are the descendants of Lilith, the first wife of Adam, who was banished from the Garden of Eden for preferring to have the dominant position with Adam during intercourse. Such an unseemly display of female power was threatening to men. The repressive attitude of medieval churchmen toward sex spurred succubi into wreaking havoc with mortal men's dreams, prompting the conflicting feelings of pleasure, pain, and fear of eternal hellfire in pious, Christian men.

Nowadays the threat of the succubus and her demon brother, the incubus, is not as sexually based as it once was (much to the chagrin, no doubt, of dreamers everywhere). The conflicting emotions they induce, however, are the same. Their nocturnal visitations are reminders that all is not well in the murky recesses of the sleeper's mind. Interpreting one's dreams can be as difficult as trying to make sense of a visit to the fairy realm. But in order for healing to begin, people who are frequently visited by the succubus must dig deep into their psyches and expose unwelcome aspects of their true nature. The succubus teaches us that in order to move out of darkness, mortals must learn to face their fears and name them.

The Succubus' Tale

THERE WAS A TOWN WITH many names in a great land of many tongues where a man called Jacob Masterson lived. He was an important man in the town where he dwelt, for he served on the town council and helped maintain order and the smooth running of the citizens' affairs.

Jacob Masterson had a dutiful wife, whose name was Mary, and two children; a boy first, and then a girl, which was just as it should be. Bearing her second child was burdensome for Mary, so she required much bed rest and care. Jacob sought the help of a midwife, Flora Wicks by name, to look after his wife. Flora tended to Mary for many weeks before she delivered, bringing herbs and tinctures to ease Mary through her time.

Jacob watched Flora as she came every day to care for his wife and marveled at her gentle, healing ways. Her eyes were soft and deep, and seemed to possess an ancient wisdom far beyond her years. And so it came to pass that Jacob's admiration for Flora turned to desire, and he became sorely troubled.

One night, as Mary's time drew near, Jacob writhed in his bed, desperate to express his desire. But because he was mostly a good man, he let his wife be. When at last he fell into a fitful slumber, a vision appeared to him. There, at the foot of the bed, stood Flora Wicks. She wore naught but a silver chain around her neck, which she twirled between her fingers. Her long hair was undone and lay about her shoulders in a tumult of curls. But her eyes were not so soft as he had known them, for she seemed to look right through him, and know what was in his soul. As he gazed upon her comely form, his fear grew equal to his desire.

Flora spoke not a word as she crept onto the bed, right over the sleeping Mary and onto the quivering body of Jacob Masterson. She sat astride his body and caressed him fondly. Jacob did not resist her but moaned softly as she rode him until he was spent. When he awoke with a start, Flora had gone.

Flora continued to visit Mary by day and Jacob by night. Soon Jacob's respect for her turned to contempt, because her presence incited him to sin. When Mary gave birth at last to a beautiful baby girl, Jacob was proud and relieved. Flora no longer came to call, and for a little while Jacob slept soundly again.

After the birth of her daughter, Mary, who tended her babies with great devotion, was too exhausted to do her duty by her husband.

"No matter," thought Jacob, "she will be my wife in body as well as soul when she is rested and whole again."

But Jacob was filled with desire and his loins burned like the fires of hell. One day, when he spied Flora Wicks in the town, he did not greet her and turned away in dread. But that night the midwife came to him again, until he lay exhausted and in great fear. Flora Wicks persisted with her visitations until Jacob knew not whether to revile or revere her. So he said nothing and kept his peace. But his lust for Flora Wicks did not abate, until one day he hated her with a passion greater than his love for his wife.

There came a day, as he was conferring with the town council, that the bishop came to speak with them.

"If there are any here who know a witch, it is your Christian duty to name her," declared the bishop. "For if you do not, you are as guilty as she for crimes against God Almighty."

"I know no witch," Jacob replied.

That night the spirit of Flora Wicks was upon him again, so that when he awoke his heart was filled with fear and loathing, and he understood that he had been consorting with a witch.

"She has tempted me from the path of righteousness for the last time," he resolved, and went straight to the bishop: "I do know a woman who is an evil temptress and a witch, and her name is Flora Wicks."

Flora Wicks was arrested that same day. She was tortured until she confessed to consorting with the devil, whereupon she was sentenced to burn at the stake. There was great consternation in the town on the day that Flora Wicks was to burn, for she had been well-loved by the townsfolk. Jacob watched as the flames engulfed and consumed Flora Wicks, who cried out in pain and terror. He smiled faintly as she burned: at last he would be able to sleep undisturbed.

That night, as the charred remains of Flora Wicks were removed from the pyre, Jacob Masterson felt an uneasy peace as he prepared for bed. At the stroke of midnight, as he slumbered next to Mary, the vision of Flora Wicks came to him again.

SHINSEEN

Immortality

THE DIMINUTIVE FAIRIES OF ANCIENT Chinese legend, the Shinseen, bear many similarities to the fairy folk of Europe. They are a mostly benign, delicate, exquisite species of fairy that live in the forests and mountains of China. Like many of their counterparts in the rest of the fairy world, they are shapeshifters and have been known to appear in the form of elderly men with long beards. It has been noted that these forest-dwelling fairies have a fondness for playing the noble game of chess.

The following story is an excellent illustration of some of the most notable similarities in the numerous global concepts that exist of the Otherworld. The most prominent fairy feature of the story is the concept of time in fairy land. Some mortals wish to live forever; this unrealistic desire can be fulfilled if they find themselves caught in the Otherworld. Fairies, being immortal, do not experience time in the linear fashion that mortals do. What may appear to be a few hours or days in the Otherworld may be hundreds of years in human time. But if a mortal returns from the fairy realm to this world, he or she quickly ages and dies, usually disintegrating into a heap of dust.

The misplaced human desire for immortality is not uncommon. Such wishful thinking denies the true essence of mortal existence and usually leads to dissatisfaction with the here and now. By living fully and mindfully in the present, a person can create a legacy of good works and deeds that will continue to have beneficial effects long after the body has ceased to be.

The Shinseen's Tale

Liu Chu'an and Yuan Chao were cousins and the best of friends. They were both very good boys and the pride of their respective families. One sunny summer's day the boys went on an errand to fetch water from a mountain spring. It was a glorious day and full of the promise of good things to come. The scent of sweet flowers and melodious birdsong filled the air. Most wondrous of all were a pair of exquisite butterflies, the size of small birds, that fluttered around the boys, as if inviting them to follow.

The young lads were enchanted and completely forgot about their errand. They followed the wayward path of the butterflies instead. Over mossy hills and through fragrant valleys they roamed until at last they arrived at a small clearing in the woods, which revealed a cave in the side of a mountain.

Before the mouth of the cave sat two fairies playing chess on the grass. Had it not been for the fairies' splendid butterfly wings, the boys would have assumed they were beautiful mortal princesses playing in the woods, for chess was a popular game among the nobility and was played regularly at court.

Although Liu Chu'an and Yuan Chao were of humble birth, they had been brought up to be respectful and courteous, so they did not disturb the lovely fairies immersed in their game of chess. The boys watched the proceedings at a proper distance, concealed behind a eucalyptus tree. Next to the fairy maidens was a restless white hare, who never ceased jumping up and down in a wide circle. Every time the hare leapt up into the air all the flowers and trees would burst into bloom, but whenever it landed on the ground and lay still for a moment, everything would suddenly wither and die, until the hare jumped again. As this strange cycle of events repeated itself over and over again, the fairy maidens continued to play chess, apparently oblivious to everything but the game. It wasn't until a couple of hours later, when the game was finally over, that the fairies took notice of the young boys.

"How long have you been watching us?" inquired one of the maidens. Yuan Chao replied that they had been there for about two hours and that it was time they returned home.

"Oh no, you mustn't do that," the fairies clamored. "Stay here with us."

But the boys were good sons and insisted that they were expected at home. Nothing the fairy maidens said could dissuade the boys from returning to their families. When it was obvious to the fairies that the boys were leaving the grotto, they gave each boy a long, slender reed. The fairies told the boys that should they ever wish to come back to the woods, they need only point their reeds at the rock where they presently stood, and the cave would open up for them. Then the fairies gathered up their chess game and walked very sadly and slowly into the cave. As soon as the fairies had disappeared into the darkness, the mouth of the cave closed over, so that only a solid mass of rock remained in its place.

The two friends hastened back to their village. But once there, they were no longer certain it was their home. Nothing looked the same. Where once was a prosperous village of fine shops and homes, now there stood only a few tumbledown, moss-covered huts. Outside one of the huts sat a couple of decrepit, aged men. The boys approached the men with deference, and introduced themselves.

"How dare you make sport of us!" exclaimed the old men. "We are the descendants of Liu Chu'an and Yuan Chao. They were our venerable ancestors four hundred years ago this day."

The boys were incredulous at such an improbable tale and insisted, as politely as they could, on the truth of the matter. Eventually, several more enfeebled old men joined the first two and soundly beat the boys for their insolence. Poor Lin Chu'an and Yuan Chao returned to the woods, chastened and bewildered. Remembering what the lovely fairies had told them, they decided to return to the fairy grotto, albeit with heavy hearts. But the boys had lost the magical reeds given to them by the fairies, for they had no way of knowing how important they would be.

The two boys beat against the rocky wall of the fairy cave to no avail, until at last they crumbled into a heap of dust. Their blissful hours at the fairy grotto had robbed them of their whole lives, because they did not know that the white hare they had watched with such fascination was the Fairy Hare of the Seasons—every time it jumped another season would pass. Thus did the young boys watch hundreds of mortal years roll by as the fairy maidens played a quiet game of chess.

CAILLEACH BHEUR

Rebirth

T HERE ARE MANY LOCAL VARIATIONS and legends throughout Scotland and Ireland of the Cailleach Bheur (pronounced kalyach vare). In the Highlands of Scotland she is depicted as a blue-faced hag who dresses in plaid and carries a staff. Her seasonal domain is the winter, from Samhain Eve (Hallowe'en) to Beltaine Eve (May Day Eve). In the winter the Cailleach Bheur commands the elements, stunting the growth of plants and creating harsh weather and snow. When her time of rule comes to an end, she throws her staff under a holly tree or a gorse bush and turns into stone, although some people claim she transforms herself into a fair maiden, personifying spring. There are a number of standing stones in the highlands and islands of Scotland dedicated to the Cailleach. Vestiges of her former status as a pagan goddess are reflected in her role as guardian of wells, streams, and wild animals, especially deer. Some of her legends describe how she is responsible for the creation of natural formations, such as rocky cliffs, mountains, and lakes.

Although the figure of Cailleach Bheur represents winter and the passing of life into cold, barren earth, she also signifies rebirth and new beginnings. Her appearance every winter is a natural and necessary part of the cycle of the seasons. It is hard for mortals to accept the passing of time because they have lost touch with the rhythms of nature. In the natural world, winter is a time of rest and regeneration. The Cailleach reminds us that death is not an end but a transition and rite of passage.

The Cailleach Bheur's Tale

NOBODY IS COMPLETELY sure how the Cailleach Bheur feels about her lot in life. How could they? She is immortal. Ordinary folk do not know of such things. But there are still those who would venture their opinion; some say she feels great glee in bringing about the chilly winds and snows of winter and beating down all green, growing things. She enjoys the death and desolation she causes when she creates natural disasters, why else would she be so hideous-looking? No doubt her face is blue because she's perpetually cold, both from within and without. Many are the tales of her wanton destruction of the Summer Maiden, who is her captive in a cavern beneath Ben Nevis, for no more reason than jealousy.

But other folk, who claim to understand the Cailleach, say she's not really so bad. The Cailleach does what she does because it is her nature. When she raises great storms to keep the Summer Maiden from arriving, it is a matter of survival. Nature has always been thus. The Cailleach Bheur does not act out of spite and has been known to feel remorse for the destruction she has caused, whether it had been deliberate or otherwise. Whatever the truth may be, all nature is struck in a profound way when she visits every winter.

There was a time when the Cailleach was guardian of the well on top of Ben Cruachan in the Scottish Highlands. Every evening before the sun set it was her duty to dam the flow of the well with a stone slab, then release the waters at dawn by removing it. One night, after a long day of herding her animals, she arrived at the well more weary than usual. She decided to lay upon the ground for a few minutes to catch her breath, before moving the massive boulder. Unfortunately she was so tired that she fell asleep on top of the stone, instead of placing it over the well.

While the Cailleach slept, the water continued to flow until it was pouring over the top of the fountain. By midnight the waters were gushing down the mountainside and flooding the valley below. She must have been very tired indeed, for although she had been sleeping with frigid, mountain waters swirling all around her, she did not awake until the sound of the rushing waters burst a dam in one of the narrow passes down in the valley. By that time many animals had been drowned in the raging flood, including the herd of goats she had driven for many miles that very day.

She watched in horror as the carcasses of deer, boar, wild cattle, and goats were swept away by the rushing waters out of the valley and on to the plains. All her attempts to stop the deluge from doing further damage were in vain. A number of small farms had once dotted the valley and surrounding pastures but all evidence of human habitation had been completely wiped out. It was obvious to the Cailleach that there had been considerable loss of human life as well. All that remained was a deep, vast stretch of water.

By daybreak the flooding had finally subsided. The chaos that had ruled the night was gone. In its place was an uneasy quiet. No birds sang. No wind stirred. The still surface of the waters concealed the devastation beneath. Where once there had been forest and field, rocks and trees, crops and cattle, there now lay a deep mountain lake, fed by the frigid waters of Ben Cruachan.

There is no other explanation for what happened next, except to say that the Cailleach felt great remorse for the destruction that her negligence had caused. She gazed upon the scene that lay before her in much fear and wonder. As if waiting for a solution to the injury she had done to suddenly dawn on her, she did not move from where she stood. The vivid blue color of her face drained into the lake beneath her, leaving her parched and pale. She remained fixed in this position for many days until at last all that was left of her was stone.

The Cailleach stands overlooking the loch to this day. You can see her stone image if you go to Loch Awe in the highlands of Scotland. It has been said that the crystal blue waters of the loch were made by the color that drained from the Cailleach's face. Other people say that the beauty of the surroundings is awe-inspiring and gave the loch its name. But that is only part of the truth. As she surveyed her creation from the summit of Ben Cruachan, the last thing she felt before she turned to stone was an overwhelming sense of dread.

GRUAGACH

Gratitude

THE GRUAGACH OF THE SCOTTISH Highlands sometimes appears as a beautiful woman with long, golden hair but more frequently is an old hag in clothes that are dripping wet, no doubt due to her predilection for running water. Her name comes from the Scots Gaelic word for "hairy," which describes one of her more disconcerting features, but she can also be identified by her weathered, green clothes and the shepherd's staff which she carries. She is a solitary fairy, who performs brownie-type activities for her benefactors, especially the herding of cattle. Mortals who are able to look past her grotesque appearance and treat her with kindness are rewarded but, true to her fairy nature, she punishes those who abuse her by stealing their cattle and putting a blight on their crops so that they are ruined.

Gruagach's lesson is about learning to feel grateful for the ordinary, daily blessings we so often take for granted. Gratitude is easy to come by when we are blessed with unexpected good fortune, happy endings, or grand events. But to feel genuine gratitude is to appreciate all the small, seemingly insignificant miracles that happen every day. Feel the wonder of simply reading words written on a page, and note how thoughts follow. Stop and think how different your life would be if you were unable to read. Having a few moments just to read these words is another reason for gratitude.

Ordinary magic is all around you all the time. Recognize it. Enjoy it. Express it. That is gratitude.

Gruagach's Tale

GRUAGACH WAS TIRED of walking. The roads were hard and dusty and her feet were sore. She loved travelling far and wide around the countryside, but sometimes harsh conditions necessitated another mode of transportation. She strayed from the stony road and walked straight through farmer MacFarlane's fields to the nearest stream. Cows grazing in the fields stopped for a moment and greeted Gruagach with gentle lowing. A newborn calf loped up to her side and nuzzled the hem of her long, green robes.

"Sorry, my sweet, no milk, today," said the hag to the baby animal. The calf stared up at her with large, brown, adoring eyes. He didn't want milk, his mother had plenty to spare. He wanted to follow Gruagach wherever she went. Gruagach put out a gnarled, bony hand to stroke the calf's ears.

"Not today, my sweet," she purred. "Some other time, perhaps." Then Gruagach planted a parting kiss on his muzzle.

Gruagach made her way across the field until she came to a stream that overflowed with water from the mountains. This pleased Gruagach very much, so in she jumped. Gruagach surrendered herself to the gushing currents and hummed a carefree tune as she floated downstream. She used her walking staff to keep herself from bumping into rocks and fallen trees as her voluminous skirts billowed about her in the water. What a sight she was to behold! She passed by a young lad as he fished on the bank of the stream, but all he saw was a tangle of twigs and weeds floating by.

Her journey ended when she was washed ashore at Pook's Pond. Since she had no business there, she hurried on her way. She stumbled through bush and briar until she came to a road that led straight to Angus McKay's. When Angus opened the door to Gruagach's pleas for help, he gasped aloud, and none too politely either. Before him stood a bedraggled old woman of more years than anyone had the right to live.

"May I warm myself by your fire, good sir?" she begged. Angus had a lot on his mind—the calfing season, sowing the hay, and a newborn son. He gave his answer without so much as a word: slam went the door in Gruagach's face. Gruagach ignored the splinters at the end of her nose and pondered Angus's mean-spirited actions.

"It does not bode well for the crofter McKay," mused Gruagach, as she surveyed his fine herd of Highland cattle. Without further ado Gruagach set out across his fields, cutting right through the middle of the herd. By the time she reached the road she had a dozen fat and willing cattle in tow.

The sun was low on the western horizon as she approached the neighboring farm. The cattle followed her without needing to be coaxed. Passers-by only saw clouds of dust being stirred up by small gusts of wind where the cattle trod.

At the next farmhouse, Gruagach stood for a moment on the threshold before banging on the door with her staff. A young girl opened the door and gazed up at Gruagach, more curious than afraid. Gruagach appealed to the child for a seat by the fire and a mug of warm milk.

"Dada," said the girl, "there's an old woman who needs a fire to warm herself by."

"Bring her in then, lass," Gruagach heard the father reply.

The farmer's wife prepared a mug of warm milk while the daughter showed Gruagach a stool by the hearth. The hag was most grateful for their kindness, and after much fuss and comforting, fell asleep. The farmer instructed his wife and daughter to leave her be. She remained seated upright on the stool but her eyes were shut and she snored loudly, so asleep she must have been.

"Must be a fairy woman," the crofter's daughter concluded.

The following morning the farmer and his family awoke and found Gruagach gone. The only reminder of her visit was the empty mug next to the hearth, which had been swept clean. The farmer, being a practical man, had no time to ponder the whereabouts of the beggar, so he set about his daily chores at once. Much to his amazement, he found his herd of cattle already grazing in the farthest meadow, just exactly where they should have been. Even more astonishing was that he counted at least twelve more head of cattle than belonged to the herd. Being an honest man, he looked for markings to identify their owner, but found only his own stamp on every animal. That was when his thoughts turned to Gruagach again.

"Must have been a fairy woman," he observed correctly, and was grateful for Gruagach's fairy favors.

PUCK

Mirth

PUCK IS A FAIRY OF THE HOBGOBLIN type, made famous by Shakespeare in *A Midsummer Night's Dream*. Also known by the name of Robin Goodfellow, he is a good-natured, mischievous sprite, who takes great delight in playing pranks and practical jokes on unsuspecting mortals. Hobs have excellent shapeshifting abilities, which make it very easy for them to lead their hapless victims astray.

Hobgoblins are related to brownies, which may account for Puck's role as personal attendant to Oberon, King of the Otherworld. Puck also enjoys the privileges of being Oberon's fairy fool or jester. The court fool, whether it be in this world or the other, may speak freely to the king on most matters, without fear of reprisal. Such is the role of an outsider in an outsider's world.

Puck illustrates the importance of laughter and fun. It is fairy medicine for the mortal soul. Mirth allows the inner child to come out and play, unafraid and unapologetic. A daily dose of mirth puts ordinary problems into perspective. Dour, mirthless individuals are frequently the butt of fairy jokes.

A healthy, well-adjusted life is often the gift of mortals who recognize their own folly and are able to find humor in it. Fairy folk hold a mortal's ability to laugh at him or herself in high regard, for fairies relish making sport of human folly. Not surprisingly, a quote from the Bard explains Puck's lesson best:

"Let me play the fool, with mirth and laughter let old wrinkles come."

Puck's Tale

Oberon, King of Fairydom, Lord of the Realm, was having a bad day. His quarrel with Titania, his consort and queen, had lasted long enough and was creating chaos in the mortal realm.

Oberon was smitten with a young Indian prince who was Titania's charge. The fairy queen was the guardian of the beautiful changeling boy, whom she adored with an ardor equal to Oberon's. For the sake of the child's deceased mother, whom she had loved like a sister, Titania would not give up the boy.

The trouble between the two sovereigns of nature had caused storms, floods, and frost. Natural forces expressed the anger that Titania and Oberon bore for each other. The land that had flourished with their union now crumbled because of their strife. Ordinary mortals began to suffer famine and disease.

And now Oberon suffered too. Titania had withdrawn her favors from him ever since they had first quarrelled, and he could bear it no longer. So he summoned Puck, his fairy fool, to help relieve him of his distress.

But Puck was busy elsewhere, revelling in his impish nature. It was only after he had charmed an exhausted housewife into endlessly churning ale, without result of barm or beer, that he answered his lord.

"Tarry not when I am so bothered, Lob. Amuse me anon," commanded Oberon.

Upon spying the fairy king, Puck knew at once why he had been called, for Oberon was unable to conceal the reason for his discontent. Puck winked slyly at Oberon.

"You bear a great load, my lord. But I will relieve thee of thy burden," he assured the king. Thus Puck began to tell a tale to distract Oberon. The knavish sprite spoke of his nightly adventures and how he would cause foolish mortals, who wandered in the woods, to lose all sense of direction.

"This does naught for me," shouted Oberon impatiently. "See how I am unmoved and stiff with anger?"

"Methinks thou hast taken a mirth-control pill, my lord," quipped the sprite to his master. Puck detected a faint smirk lurking beneath the surface of Oberon's somber visage.

Puck changed swiftly into the form of a young dappled mare. The fairy filly danced and whinnied for the king, who was not amused.

"She is too small to ride my stallion," grumbled the king with satisfaction. He would learn to play Puck's game.

"She is not for you, sire," answered the puckish mare. "But see what comes here."

Puck swung his mane in the direction of a fat, slobbering, old horse that loped into the forest clearing, where Puck and Oberon stood. The horse snorted a feeble greeting, to which Puck responded with much prancing all around the beast, driving him dizzy with desire. But Puck soon wearied of his game and vanished. The horse paid no heed; for he turned about in little circles, twisted front to back, with only his tail to chase.

"This steed will have no tail today!" roared Oberon, his sides aching from laughter.

"It is most unseemly for a king to laugh at another's misfortune," said Puck, who suddenly had materialized astride the woebegone horse.

"I laugh at my own," replied Oberon, "it softens my hardship." Puck took a closer look at the fairy king and noticed that he spoke the truth. "Your game was well-played, good Master Puck. Mark you, make no beast of me, lest ye be made the fool," advised the fairy king to his bold minion.

"Not for thee, sire, would I be so foolish. When there be another time, I will find a worthy fool," Puck replied.

"So long as it serve me well, gentle Puck," cried Oberon, as he took the form of a great hawk. "I shall keep this guise awhile. For mark, here comes my lady."

Titania and her great numbers of trooping fairies entered the forest glen. There was a great commotion all around, as all nature cooed and glowed. No mortal eyes beheld the sight. Thus began another night.

SIDHE

Beauty

THE SIDHE (PRONOUNCED SHEE) are the descendants of the ancient inhabitants of Ireland, the Tuatha de Danaan. Formally known as the Daoine (pronounced Deena) Sidhe, they are seen to be the aristocracy of the fairy realm in a small country that boasts one of the largest fairy populations in the world.

The Sidhe are a heroic race of fairies reputed for their aristocratic bearing and beauty. They are a tall, elegant host of immortals with long, luxurious hair and are usually seen dressed in shining white garments. Their talents for music and dance are unparalleled in the mortal world. After the conquering Milesians supplanted them as the ruling peoples of Ireland, the Sidhe retreated into grassy mounds and hills, where they dwell to this day. (*Sidhe* is Irish for mound.)

As the nobility of the Celtic Otherworld, the Sidhe are accustomed to being surrounded with evershifting, sometimes frightening, beauty. Their fondness for music and dance demonstrates an appreciation for beauty in all its myriad forms. They live, work, fight, and play with sumptuous abandon, relishing each moment and detail of their rich, volatile existences.

Beauty is not always present in a form recognized by the five mortal senses. More often than not it is a deliberate choice, a way of being. When hidden or disguised, beauty must be sought out and revealed. Beauty exists even in the most offensive or distressing situations, as long as there is a wish for it. If you cannot see it right away, time will eventually reveal the beauty you did not immediately recognize, that was unconsciously kept deep within you.

The Sidhe's Tale

THE DAY KATY O'CONNOR was born was the happiest day of her mother's life. She was a healthy, beautiful baby with soft, wispy red curls that ran riot all over her tiny, newborn head. Her mother took one look at her darling daughter and declared that Katy's head full of crimson curls was a tempting place for the fairies to run amok. Katy was most surely marked as a very special and gifted child.

Most notable of all was Katy's capacity for great joy and laughter. She was blessed with a cheerful disposition that not even the rudest, meanest people or circumstances could spoil. She found joy where no one else could, and then shared it with everyone. Her presence alone was a gift.

Many good things were predicted for Katy. She would grow up to be a lovely young woman and make some man very happy, and of course she would be the sweetest and kindest of mothers and raise many fine children. But that was never to be. She was still a young girl when the course of her life was changed forever.

The sun hovered just above the green mountains of Connaught, where she lived, after a day of serious play with two of her childhood friends. The thin wisps of smoke rising from the chimneys in the village nestled in the valley below told the children that supper was on the hearth and it was time to go. The youthful trio began their walk home when Katy realized she had forgotten the pouch of pretty stones she had found. With an admonition to her friends to wait for her, Katy ran back to the clearing at the edge of the woods where they had spent the day.

Sure enough, Katy found her pouch just exactly where she had left it. She was about to return to her friends when she heard the sound of the faintest tinkling of bells carried on a sudden gust of wind. Katy stood quietly in rapt attention as the sound of the bells grew louder, sweeter, and closer all the time.

"There is some magic afoot," Katy thought with glee. All at once she spied a pale-green light shining from deep within the forest. Moments later a troop of handsome people dressed in exquisite garments of green and gold emerged from the thicket. They danced and sang as they threw fragrant pink and purple flower petals all around. The green light in the woods grew increasingly brighter as Katy gazed upon the scene in wonder. Then another group, bedecked in finery more beautiful than the previous company, entered the clearing. They rode magnificent white horses with golden bridles decorated with jingling, jangling bells. Atop all the horses there rode men and women of regal bearing. Their hair shone golden-red in the fading sun and their brilliant, silver-white robes radiated light. Some of the riders held glittering blue swords in their upraised arms.

The revellers took no notice of Katy as they rode by. She did not move from where she stood until the jubilant throng had disappeared into the woods that lay across the meadow. Katy's wonder did not subside. She was still quite awestruck and uncharacteristically subdued when her friends found her standing in the clearing alone. They knew at once that something strange had befallen their friend. Although she stood before them, quite solid and real, somehow she was no longer there.

And that was how Katy remained for the rest of her life. She was always gentle and kind, but the exuberance of her childhood was gone forever. She kept to herself and pondered the mysteries of nature and life much more than most ordinary folk do. Her family and friends tried their best to shake Katy from her wistful reverie, but to no avail. She longed for the beauty and magic she had known when the Otherworldly host had crossed her path a lifetime before.

Katy never married. Despite her sweet nature, she was too melancholy and distracted to make a suitable wife and mother. Besides, everyone knew that there wasn't a mortal man alive who could make her happy. Katy became stranger and more distant as the years went by until one day she was a very lonely old spinster about whom many stories were made up and told.

There came a day when Katy knew she had lived in this world long enough. So she set about preparing herself for bed more carefully than usual. Before retiring, she looked longingly at her beloved mountains, as if seeking a sign. That night, she died peacefully in her sleep. She was found in bed, wearing her finest clothes and a broad smile. She had never looked so happy since the day she came back from the woods with her friends so long ago. Stranger still were all the pink and purple flower petals spread about the room where she lay.

BIBLIOGRAPHY

Arrowsmith, Nancy, and Moorse, George,
A Field Guide to the Little People,
London: MacMillan, 1977.

Bierhorst, John (ed.), *The Deetkatoo:*
Native American Stories About Little People,
New York: William Morrow and Company, Inc., 1998.

Bonnet, Leslie, *Chinese Fairy Tales*,
London: Frederick Muller Limited, 1958.

Briggs, Katherine, *An Encyclopedia of Fairies:*
Hobgoblins, Brownies, Bogies and Other Supernatural Creatures,
New York: Pantheon, 1976.

—*The Vanishing People: Fairy Lore and Legends*,
New York: Pantheon, 1978.

Croker, Thomas Crofton, *Fairy Legends and Traditions*
of the South of Ireland, London: John Murray, 1825.

Curcija-Prodanovic, Nada, *Yugoslav Folk-Tales*,
London: Oxford University Press, 1957.

Evans-Wentz, W.Y., *The Fairy-Faith in Celtic Countries*,
Secaucus, New Jersey: University Books, 1966.

Harris, Christie, *Mouse Woman and the Mischief-Makers*,
Toronto: McClelland and Stewart Ltd, 1977.

Keightley, Thomas, *The World Guide to Gnomes,*
Fairies, Elves and Other Little People,
New York: Avenel Books, 1978.
(Originally published as *The Fairy Mythology*, 1880.)

Kirk, Robert, *The Secret Commonwealth of*
Elves, Fauns and Fairies, Stirling, Scotland: Eneas Mackay, 1933.

Leach, Maria (ed.), *Funk & Wagnalls'*
Standard Dictionary of Folklore, Mythology and Legend,
New York: Funk & Wagnalls, 1949.

MacManus, Dermot, *The Middle Kingdom: The Faerie*

World of Ireland, Buckinghamshire: Colin Smythe Ltd, 1973.

Mack, Carol K., and Mack, Dinah, *A Field Guide*
to Demons: Fairies, Fallen Angels and Other Subversive Spirits,
New York: Henry Holt and Company, LLC, 1998.

Malory, Thomas, *Le Morte d'Arthur*,
London: J.M. Dent & Sons Ltd, 1906.

Opie, Iona and Peter, *The Classic Fairy Tales*,
New York: Oxford University Press, 1974.

Ozaki, Yei Theodora (ed.), *The Japanese Fairy Book*,
Rutland, Vermont: Charles E. Tuttle Co. Inc., 1970.

Phillpotts, Beatrice, *The Book of Fairies*,
New York: Ballantine Books, 1979.

Rose, Carol, *Spirits, Fairies, Leprechauns, and Goblins:*
An Encyclopedia, New York: W.W. Norton & Co., 1998.

Shakespeare, William, *Complete Works*,
London: Oxford University Press, 1905.

Spence, Lewis, *British Fairy Origins: The Genesis and Development of Fairy*
Legends in British Tradition,
Wellingborough, Northamptonshire: The Aquarian Press Limited, 1981.

Walker, Barbara G., *The Woman's Dictionary of Symbols and Sacred Objects*,
San Francisco: Harper & Row, Publishers, 1988.

—*The Woman's Encyclopedia of Myths and Secrets*,
San Francisco: Harper & Row, 1983.

Werner, E.T.C., *Myths and Legends of China*,
Singapore: Graham Brash (PTE) Ltd, 1984.

Yeats, William Butler, *Mythologies*,
New York: Collier Books, 1959.

The publishers wish to thank the following for permission to reproduce
copyright material: Image Bank: pp. 15, 47, 51, 55, 59, 63, 79, 111,
127; Tony Stone: pp. 43, 99, 107, 115, 118, 123.